Vegetable Gardening Made Easy

How To Grow More Food With Less Effort

By Mitch Baylis

Copyright

Dedication

To my Opa who spent countless afternoons showing me how to grow vegetables the way his father showed him. Thanks for starting me on this journey and getting me hopelessly *Obsessed With Dirt.*

Free Book Resources

As part of your purchase you've got access to exclusive book bonuses and extras. These include printable plans for the chicken tractor, homemade fertilizer recipe, a quick start checklist to begin your first patch and many more free resources.

Plus you'll get unreleased bonuses that aren't in this book including:

- Printable plant spacing tables
- List of recommended seed companies
- Natural pest management plants list
- Plans for building an insect hotel
- Plans for building a chicken tractor
- Printable homemade fertilizer recipe
- Beginners quick start checklist

Download or print your free bonuses now.

Visit www.obsessedwithdirt.com/resources

Preface

In this book you'll find everything you need to get started on your backyard food growing journey including:

- The super productive way to grow vegetables in your backyard used by the most productive farms on earth
- How to never spend another minute doing backbreaking work ever again
- Why store bought fertilizers are ripping you off
- How you can make your own all natural fertilizers for practically nothing
- Why you need to forget everything you've ever been taught about vegetable gardening to grow the best vegetables you've ever tasted
- The one technique that will revolutionize your vegetable garden and help you grow more nutrient dense food than you ever thought possible
- The little known secret that practically eliminates all the pests and diseases from your garden overnight without using any harmful chemicals or sprays

At Obsessed With Dirt we're on a mission to help 1 million families grow all their food in their own backyards by 2050. By growing your own food not only are you feeding your body with the most nutrient dense food on the planet, but you're also making the biggest impact on global warming and sustainability of our future.

Backyard food growers like you and me are the key to feeding a world of 8 billion hungry people when the oil resources boom dries up. It's no secret that the way we've been growing food for the last hundred years is destroying our planet.

90% of our old growth forests have been cut down to grow annual monocrops of corn and soy using fertilizers made from petroleum. These chemical fertilizers systematically kill all the life in the soil until nothing is left.

So it's no wonder that farmers need to use so many chemicals to control weeds, pests and diseases that quickly spread across fields of genetically identical plants growing in fields of dead soil.

But what's more alarming is that farms all over the world are losing inches of topsoil each and every year. It's that topsoil, the rich black dirt, that is the secret to growing healthy, nutrient dense food without chemical fertilizers.

By the time petroleum runs out all the topsoil on our farms will be gone and large populations of the world will starve. Some argue that we are already starving. The near tasteless food we're growing today is far less nutritious than it was 100 years ago because we've already destroyed so much of our soil.

That's why we're Obsessed With Dirt.

And we hope that by the end of this ebook you will be too because it's the secret to growing food in your backyard the *easy way*, the way nature intended it to be.

Table Of Contents

Why You Need This Book

Before the 20th century most families lived on or near a farm. Practically everything we needed to survive came from our backyard gardens. Food, fuel, medicine and shelter, were all sourced right from our back door steps and we did it all without tractors, fertilizers and irrigation systems.

Today's vegetable gardens are more frankenscience than natural growing systems. The methods of backyard farming that have been passed down for thousands of years have been lost in just one generation.

What's more, we've all been fed one big lie about growing our own food. We're told that growing vegetables and fruits is difficult and time consuming. That we need to follow complex planting plans and tend to our gardens regularly to keep pests, diseases and weeds in check.

But as you'll discover in the coming pages growing your own food can be easy, pleasurable and can save you a great deal of money in the process.

Simple gardening methods and techniques are all that's needed to grow an abundant supply of food in your garden. You don't need to import 'good' topsoil and you don't need to spend thousands on fancy equipment or fertilizers either.

Much of what you've been taught about vegetable gardening has been a lie.

Traditional vegetable gardening methods that have sustained civilization for 10,000 years have been pushed aside and labelled as 'inefficient' and 'outdated' and replaced with intensive agriculture.

But I ask you, is intensive agriculture really more efficient?

The gardening methods described in this book will thrive on neglect, require minimal compost, water and fertilizer, and grow crops naturally resistant to pests and diseases. These gardens will grow healthy vegetables that have 120% higher antioxidant, 10.4x more nutrients[1] and a depth of flavor unmatched by anything you've ever tasted before.

Compare that to intensive agriculture which requires daily irrigation, frequent tilling, weekly fertilizing, and pest, disease and weed management. Intensive agriculture not only costs significantly more to grow crops but the food you do manage to harvest will be severely weakened, sickly and nutrient deprived.

What you're about to discover will go against all the mainstream advice you've ever been told about growing vegetables. This book won't make any friends with the big fertilizer conglomerates, agriculture companies or garden centers, but it will show you exactly how to grow your own food easily, affordably and without the use of any chemicals.

[1] *Based on the Antioxidative and antimutagenic activities study published in The Science Of Food and Agriculture Journal comparing organic vegetables to those that were conventionally grown.*

Other similar studies:

Fruit and soil quality of organic and conventional strawberry farms

Higher antioxidant and lower cadmium concentrations

Extracts from organically and conventionally cultivated strawberries

Becoming Obsessed With Dirt

I started my first vegetable garden when I was 7 years old.

Each month my mother had 2-3 gardening magazines delivered to our house. She'd sift through them for ideas for her garden. She wasn't interested in growing vegetables but she loved her roses and the lush green lawn in our front yard.

Every so often the magazine would come with a seed packet glued to the cover and my mother, who never threw anything out, had built up a collection of hundreds of these little seed packets over the years.

One day I decided to 'borrow' mums box of seeds to plant a vegetable garden. I raced outside, grabbing a few old garden tools and a watering can, found an empty spot in the garden and started digging.

I wasn't quite sure why I needed to dig the dirt over but I knew that's what I was supposed to do, so I did it. I pulled the weeds, dug over the dirt and ripped open a dozen seed packets throwing them excitedly over the dirt...

And then I waited.

I sat there all afternoon and waited for them to grow. Eventually it got dark and mum called me in for dinner.

The next day I ran home after school, dropped my bag inside and raced excitedly into our backyard to see how big my vegetable garden had grown...

Still nothing.

After about a week I gave up, but the drive to grow my

own food never disappeared. Every few years I'd try again. My vegetable gardens back then never amounted to much. I was lucky if I could harvest a handful of tomatoes over the whole season. One year I even managed to kill radishes!

I finally got serious in 2001 and went all out, spending thousands of dollars on a rototiller, top of the range fertilizers and sprays. That summer I spent every weekend out in my patch tilling the soil, adding compost, mulching, watering, fertilizing, spraying and weeding my garden.

After all my hard work (and thousands of dollars later) I finally had a vegetable garden that actually produced something! Hallelujah!

But growing my own vegetables quickly turned into a very expensive hobby. Every year at the start of the season I'd rototill my whole plot. The soil seemed to get harder every year and needed more tilling to lighten up but it worked, so I kept on tilling.

After the beds were tilled, I'd bring in a truckload of high quality compost from the soil yard and mix it into my soil. Then I'd make the raised beds and setup the irrigation too. Just preparing my garden would take 3 full weekends of backbreaking work, and then I had to plant my crops!

I never bothered sowing seeds because getting them to come up was about as likely as winning the lottery. So I would just buy hundreds of little seedlings from the garden center and plant them one by one. Planting a row of a hundred seedlings would take me over an hour because I'd have to dig a little hole for every plant and then water them in.

To get my new seedlings to grow I'd also get a dozen bags of specially formulated fertilizers. Every crop had its own blend of nutrients in a handy pelletized ball that I could throw around the plants every few weeks to keep them growing fast.

After I fertilized my yard I'd set the irrigation system to water 7 days a week, morning and night! Luckily I was on my own bore water back then or the water authorities would have been knocking at my door for an explanation of my abnormally high water use.

Soon enough pests and diseases would start showing up on my crops. So I'd drive back to my garden center and buy the miracle-in-a-bottle for whatever problem I had. My car would get loaded up with hundreds of dollars worth of gear like, stakes, growing cages, snail and slug pellets, pest control, bird netting, weed sprays, special growth tonics and anything I thought would solve my garden problems.

No matter what I did, it was a never ending battle against pests and diseases. The first time I sprayed the control was great, it'd wipe them out completely. But in a few weeks they were back and this time the sprays only killed a few of them! Every time I'd have to use more and more chemicals to keep the pests under control.

What's more, every few weeks there seemed to be a new problem in my garden. One week my tomatoes would be fine, the next they all had blossom end rot. Once I fixed that they would be attacked by beetles, black spot or something else! I was forever taking trips to the garden center to buy whatever I could to keep my crops alive.

I was probably the garden centers best customer back then. By the end of the season they were all greeting me by name, and I inevitably always left with a cart full of gear for my yard.

After the first year things only got worse. My soil kept getting more compacted and I needed a more powerful tiller to work it. My plants stopped growing as well as they used to and I ended up using more fertilizers just to keep them healthy. The pests and diseases were practically laughing at my attempts to control them, they had quickly built up a tolerance for all the chemicals and were now much harder to control.

But how could this happen?

I had carefully followed everything I was supposed to do!

On the last weekend of Summer I sat down and tallied up everything I had bought for my vegetable garden over season. That year I had grown almost all tomatoes because everything else was eaten by bugs and destroyed by disease. I grew heaps of tomatoes that year, but only few hundred of them were edible, the others were filled with bugs or tasted horrible. That year I spent $753.62 to grow 214 tomatoes, which was over $3.50 per tomato!

What's worse is that most of the tomatoes didn't even taste anywhere near as good as what I could buy in the store. They were watery, tasteless and powdery. The only thing they seemed to be good for were making relishes and chutneys where could hide the lack of flavor with spices and sugar.

Growing your own food the way we're all taught is backbreaking work, super expensive and a complete waste of time. Truth is this method has been intentionally designed for you to struggle. Garden centers, magazines and suppliers promote this type of 'intensive' gardening because it sells products.

Like so many backyard gardeners I was ready to throw in the trowel and give up. But as I was about to learn there was a much easier way to grow vegetables. Afterall we had been growing them for thousands of years without fertilizers, irrigation, pest control or even tractors...

Opa's Vegetable Garden

My Opa was one of those gardeners who seemed to effortlessly grow anything. His vegetable garden was always full of huge cabbages, carrots and bright red tomatoes.

I can still remember listening to the wind rustle against the 8 foot high corn, the bees buzzing from one flower to the next and the birds chirping happily as they darted around eating bugs.

Opa had learned to grow vegetables from his father when he lived in Holland, a traditional method that had been passed down for generations in their little village. Whilst I was spending thousands on fertilizers and chemicals trying to get my garden to grow, Opa was casually enjoying the harvests from in his garden.

Everything in his yard thrived without his constant attention. He never had any pests or diseases to worry about and hardly ever worked out in his garden. I never saw him tilling his beds or spreading compost and manures. His garden just seemed to grow like *magic.*

"That? That isn't my garden!" he said whilst chuckling loudly.

Taking 3 giant steps towards the garden bed in front of us, he reached down and grabbed a fistful of black dirt. Still smiling widely he grabbed my hand and plonked the dirt onto my palm. The soil was warm and full of wriggling worms.

"This is my garden"

"I don't grow tomatoes or potatoes. I grow dirt"

"Look at it, it's more beautiful than any garden" Thrusting another handful of it towards me.

"Everything that grows and everything that you eat. It all comes from the dirt"

I looked at Opa. Still a little confused that he could grow such an incredible garden by focusing not on the plants, but on the dirt that they grew in. Opa was completely obsessed with dirt and soon I would be too.

Everything he did was for the soil. If he looked after the soil the plants would thrive because the soil would have everything they needed to grow. He didn't need to control pest and diseases because his plants never got sick. Opa didn't have to feed the plants fertilizers because all the nutrients were stored in the soil.

What really struck me though was that Opa hardly ever watered his garden. All the water his plants needed was already in the soil and his crops would thrive all through summer without any irrigation!

But could this really be possible? Could it all really be because of the soil?

Learning To Listen To Nature

"It's time for your first lesson. But you won't learn it in here" Opa said as he closed the gate behind him and started walking downhill towards the stream that ran through his property.

Whilst most 95 year old's would be cautiously hobbling along, Opa was practically jogging down the hill in excitement. When I finally caught up with him he was sitting on a large grey boulder watching the water gently flow downstream.

"What do you see over there?" he said, gesturing to the plants growing along the bank of the river.

I looked across the river to a flat area along the bank. It

didn't look like anything, the soil was black and clearly fertile, it looked better than the soil back home. Yet all I could see growing were a bunch of weeds!

"That there, that's the truth. It's all you need to know about growing vegetables"

What on earth is he talking about? What has any of this got to do with growing vegetables?

Opa slid down from the boulder and walked across to the bank of the river. He glanced his eyes over a few of the weedy looking plants growing there before pulling one up and passing it to me as he asked

"What does this look like to you?"

"A weed Opa" I responded, trying hard not to roll my eyes.

"Rub the leaves" he said as he handed the weed back to me.

"It smells like a carrot!" I gasped.

"That's because it is" he said smiling broadly.

"It's a wild carrot. Here, and this one is wild lettuce, this is wild fennel, and that, that is a wild tomato"

"There's some parsley over there, and that's a mint right there by the water"

Looking around, we were standing in a wild vegetable garden. It hadn't been planted by anyone, it was never watered, fertilized or tended and yet there were vegetables growing everywhere.

These were *wild vegetables* and they were thriving all by themselves without any gardeners looking after them, not even Opa.

"Everything you need to know about growing vegetables is right here on the river"

Each year when the river floods it brings rich silt up onto the floodplains. The flood waters rush by pulling last years plants out and pulverizing them into fine compost which settles on the banks. The river stirs up the top of the soil making it light and fluffy.

When the flood drains away the banks are fertile and fluffy. The seeds from last years vegetables are already in the soil waiting for the sun to wake them up. As the soil warms the seeds germinate and this years vegetables grow.

Many seeds germinate in the rich soil, too many to count, and that's where nature steps in to help. The weakest get eaten by bugs, those that grow too slowly get sick and die, leaving only the strongest plants to set seed for the following year.

All the vegetables we grow today have been selected from these wild vegetables. Although they may look very different, modern vegetables still behave like their wild cousins and need the same growing conditions.

Vegetables only grow for 1-2 years before setting seed and dying. They need very rich soils to support their fast growth and don't have the energy to compete against other plants. This is why you'll only find them growing in recently disturbed ground, such as along rivers or near human camps.

If you want to grow vegetables in your backyard then you need to mimic how wild vegetables naturally grow along the flood plains. Fluff up your soil once a year, grow in a rich loam (river banks are almost always loam soils, which we'll talk about later), sow directly into the beds, thin to the strongest plants, do not mulch, and water minimally.

Unfortunately even if you do live along a natural waterway chances are it will not flood anymore. Governments have installed dams and other devices to all the great rivers to stop them from flooding. This has become increasingly important as more floodplains are converted from farmland into prime real estate.

Hundreds of civilizations have grown crops for thousands of years along these rich floodplains relying on the natural ebb and flow of the river to feed and irrigate crops. Egypt which spanned more than 6,000 years thrived on the banks of the Nile. Ancient China had the Yellow river, Rome fed it's people from the Tiber and early settlers in the US relied heavily on the Mississippi for much of their farmland.

Unfortunately vegetable gardeners won't be able to rely on the river and floodplains to do all the hard work for you anymore. But you can still learn a lot from the river and how vegetables have grown for thousands of years to design a vegetable garden that thrives without your constant attention.

Planning Your Vegetable Garden

It was getting dark so Opa and I started walking back up to the house. Along the way we walked along the thicket of shrubs that hugged the river. These plants grew just out of the floodplains and were filled with flowers, animals and insects. There was a lot of life down here along the river, much more than I had realized.

Opa picked up some dry wood for the fire and handed me a handful of wild raspberries that he had picked from one of the shrubs and we headed on back to the house for dinner.

When I walked into the kitchen the nutty smell of roasted butternut squash with rosemary had filled the air. On the table was a roasted chicken, butternut squash, stuffed peppers, and a colorful tomato-cucumber salad.

Everything on the table had come from Opa's vegetable garden including the chicken. Completely blown away by all the rich flavors I asked Oma what made everything taste so good.

With a big smile she said "Plenty of sunshine"

That wasn't what I was expecting her to say at all, sunshine wasn't an ingredient. She must of used some secret herbs or something, but when I looked to Opa he simple smiled and nodded

"Sunshine is the most important nutrient for your vegetables to grow. It makes chickens taste pretty good too!"

But could the sun really make that much of a difference to how food tastes? Perhaps that's why my vegetables never tasted as good as I wanted them too. I had been so excited to start my first patch all those years ago that I never spent any time planning where it should go, I just picked somewhere and started digging.

Planning your vegetable garden and ensuring there's plenty of sunshine available is the most important step. Sunshine is the only nutrient that you can't bring into your garden with a wheelbarrow, so you better make sure you've got plenty of it already there!

I see so many vegetable gardeners setting themselves up for failure by failing to plan their gardens before they start digging them. Often what ends up happening is that they spend all their time trying to grow vegetables in a garden that doesn't get enough sun. Sometimes it's because of a big tree that shades the area, or it might just be on the wrong side of the house.

That's why the first step to starting any vegetable garden is to plan it. Draw everything out on paper before you ever start to dig. Good vegetable garden design is the difference between a garden that thrives with little care, and one that requires hundreds of hours and thousands of dollars in inputs to grow a crop.

So what is the best location for your new patch?

Choosing The Right Site For Your Vegetable Garden

Plants need a lot of sunshine to grow. Vegetables in particular will benefit from early morning sun because it warms the soil and promotes early germination and fast growth. The more sun your crops get the faster they'll grow and the healthier they'll be.

Given the choice between planting your vegetable garden where it gets afternoon sun or morning sun, you should always choose the morning sun position. Afternoon sunshine is much hotter and more likely to burn your plants leaves and dry out the soil.

The morning sun is gentler and as long as your plants still get at least 6 hours of sunshine everyday they'll continue to grow at their best. If you don't have any areas with this much sun, then you should consider joining your local community garden which will have plenty of sunny plots to choose from, or grow your vegetables in containers.

Vegetable gardens require water, nutrients and regular care too. Water and nutrients are easy to bring to a sunny plot. You can install an additional irrigation pipe and compost can be brought in by a wheelbarrow or trailer when needed.

Big trees can also be a factor as their strong roots can quickly steal nutrients from your soil. Avoid planting your garden near big trees or hedges which can also shade out your vegetable garden as the trees get older.

Wherever possible, you should position your vegetable garden as close to your kitchen as possible. If your patch is too far away you'll be discouraged in harvesting vegetables for meals as it's a long way to walk. Vegetable gardens that are a long way from the home are also more often forgotten and neglected.

Sloped areas should be avoided as soil amendments and topsoil will slide downhill every time it rains. You'll then have to collect the topsoil and redistribute it over your garden beds again which creates needless work.

If sloped areas are only available to you then spend some additional time terracing them into stepped garden rows to reduce the soil erosion. Ideally, have your resources like compost piles and manures stored or delivered at the top of the slope so you don't have to move them uphill.

Download your free vegetable garden quick start guide for beginners at www.obsessedwithdirt.com/resources

Starting Your New Vegetable Garden

My hands were covered in blisters and everything ached.

"You're doing too much" Opa contested when he saw me dragging my exhausted body to a bench under the old oak tree.

I had found the ideal spot for my new vegetable garden and spent the better part of the last weekend digging it over. The ground was so hard that I had only managed to dig an area 10 feet by 10 feet and now everything was covered in blisters.

I had big plans for my vegetable garden but Opa was right, I needed to start with something manageable. Trying to dig over a huge area of dirt without a plan was exhausting, backbreaking work that I didn't enjoy one bit.

Opa smiled broadly as he gestured for me to join him in his garden. I heaved my sore body up off the bench and reluctantly walked over. As we strolled through his garden he picked up a big oak leaf from the path and held it up to the sun. The light revealed a hidden network of veins below the surface.

"We are here" he said as he traced his finger from the stem of the leaf and out to one of the lateral veins. I looked out at his garden trying to understand what this old oak leaf had to do with his vegetable patch.

As my eyes studied the beds and paths around me I saw it. Opa had designed his entire garden following the pattern in this leaf. The main path ran right through the middle of his patch, it was wider than the other paths just like the main stem on the leaf. From the central stem there were smaller, narrower paths and between them the garden beds and plants that Opa grew.

Seeing that I had understood his lesson on planning my gardens paths he walked over to a bed and extended his arm out over the garden. His arm reached effortlessly into the middle of the bed

"This is how wide we make the garden bed. One arm length."

Something else I noticed in Opa's garden was that all the garden beds were positioned to take full advantage of the most sun possible. The end of each row pointed either North or South which meant that as the sun moved across the sky the crops cast shadows over the paths *between the rows* and didn't shade out the other plants within their row.

The sun rises in the East and sets in the West for both the Northern and Southern hemispheres. So as the sun moves across the sky your plants will shade the path on the west side of their rows and in the afternoon the shadow will move to the path on the east side of the row. Each plant shades itself during the hottest part of the day which helps to reduce transpiration and wilting.

Garden bed rows are easiest to maintain when they are 3 to 4 feet wide and no longer than 10 feet, with paths 2 feet wide between each row. Garden beds longer than 10 take forever to walk around the garden bed to get to the other side. If your bed is wider than 4 feet you'll have to step on the soil to get to tend crops in the middle of your row.

The main access path that runs down the center of your vegetable plot should be 4 feet wide instead of 2 feet and ideally paved, mulched or compacted. You'll be bringing in compost and manures, as well as taking out old crops using this main path and the extra width and firm surface allows you to maneuver faster and more easily with a heavy wheelbarrow loaded with materials.

Paths between your garden bed rows should be left as dirt and not covered or paved. They will become slightly compacted over the season from your footsteps. Uncovered paths between rows also work to extend the fertility and water holding capacity of your garden beds.

If you want a big vegetable garden, the best thing you can do is prepare your beds in blocks of 100 sq ft (10m2). This works out to be two 10 x 4 foot garden beds and one 2 x 10 foot path between them. By preparing a new garden bed every few weeks you'll also space out planting so instead of harvesting all your crops at once, you'll have a consistent supply of them over the whole season.

Digging Your Garden Beds

The first time you dig new soil is always going to be the hardest. If your soil is heavy clay then apply gypsum and water in a week or so before digging. Gypsum helps balance your soils calcium/magnesium ratio and also removes excess sodium.

Soils with too much magnesium and high levels of sodium tighten up and are hard to dig, adding calcium and removing sodium by using Gypsum is the most effective way to loosen heavy clay soils. The sulphur in Gypsum leeches away the sodium and the calcium displaces the excess magnesium.

If your soil is sandy or easy to dig then you won't need to apply any gypsum and can start digging your beds straight away. Mark out two garden beds 4 feet wide by 10 feet long either side of a path that is 2 feet wide and 10 feet long. This will give you an area of 100 sq ft.

To prepare your garden bed you'll need a long handled shovel and a heavy duty garden fork. It's important that you use high quality tools and keep the edges sharp to make working your soil as easy as possible, we'll discuss essential tools and how to sharpen them later.

Start by removing the top 2 inches of soil from the garden bed. This will remove the weeds, seeds and grass from your new garden. If it is too hard to do scrap this off with a shovel then you can use a hoe or even a rotary tiller to loosen the top of the soil. Put the sod in a mound near the garden bed as we will use it later.

Dig a trench one spade depth deep and a spade width wide along the entire length of one side of your garden bed. If your soil is too compacted then you can loosen it before digging by pushing your garden fork down into the soil. When the fork is inserted as far as it will go, wiggle it back and forth using the weight of your body to loosen the soil, then remove it and insert your spade into the loosened soil.

Put the soil from the trench into a wheelbarrow or along the edge of the bed, but keep it separate from the weedy soil we scraped off previously. Then using your garden fork loosen the soil at the bottom of the trench by pushing the fork into the soil and levering the fork back and forth to break the dirt apart.

After the first trench has been forked over add 1-2 inches of the weed mixed soil across the bottom of the trench. Start digging the next trench and move the dirt from this trench into the first, covering the layer of weeds in clean soil. Fork over the bottom of the second trench and then repeat the process until the entire garden bed has been dug over. When you get to the last trench fill it with the soil from the wheelbarrow.

If you've done this step correctly then your garden bed should now be 2-3 inches higher than the surrounding soil. The soil in the garden bed will be light and fluffy, and the majority of the weed seeds will be buried too deeply to germinate.

It's a good idea to also scrap your garden paths clear of the sod and to fork the soil over to loosen it up slightly.

You won't need to double dig your paths but if you've got compacted soil it's a good idea to loosen them with a fork to encourage your plants to grow into them as well as the beds.

Why You Should Never Use A Rotary Tiller - EVER

I have a neighbor who loves his rotary tiller. Every year he gets the shiny new machine out of his garden shed, starts it up and tills the soil in his vegetable garden. His rotary tiller makes one hell of a racket and I can always hear him yelling about it whenever he bends a blade or steers off course.

Every few years Phil loses control of the rotary tiller and takes out a fence. Last year he was unfortunate enough to have parked his truck too close to the patch and when he lost control of the tiller he also lost half his paint job!. If you've ever used one you'll know they are notoriously difficult to keep in a straight line and control.

The worst time to use a rotary tiller is when you want to open up new ground. Tilling the top 2-3 inches of sod is fairly easy and I've used a tiller many times for this purpose, but once you start going deeper the work gets considerably harder.

Heavily compacted soil needs to be opened up 1 inch at a time with the tiller. Which means you'll have to pass the same area of dirt at least 6 times to till to a depth of 6 inches! Rocks, branches and tree roots can break or seriously damage the machine too. They can lie hidden anywhere and no matter how carefully you till the garden you'll inevitably hit something that breaks your machine.

Rotary tillers are a lot of work. They require hours of maintenance, fuel, replacement parts, regular servicing and sharpening. What's worse is that after all the hard work of fluffing up your soil is done, the machine has created a hardpan of compacted soil hidden just 6 inches below.

This compacted layer forms because your rotary tiller needs something to push against as it throws and fluffs the soil. With every rotation of your tines the soil below your tiller gets pushed down and compacted.

After several years your rotary tiller will create a hardpan of compact soil that is impossible for roots to penetrate. The hardpan creates more issues than just root development though, it also reduces the drainage of your soil and increases the likelihood of nutrients building up to toxic levels in your garden.

Every time you till your soil with a rotary machine you lose valuable organic matter and destroy soil life. Most tillers operate at 540 RPM which means the tiller blades are tearing through your garden soil at a frighteningly fast pace that no earthworm or insect can outpace.

What you're left with is a compacted subsoil, with an overly aerated topsoil that has been stripped of all soil life and had the majority of the organic matter blown away in the wind with each pass of the tiller.

Digging and forking over your garden soil may seem like a time consuming task but when you add up all the additional time and expense a rotary machine *creates* in your garden, hand turning beds is considerably more efficient.

The Battle Between Raised Beds And Inground Rows

Raised bed gardens have really taken off in recent years. Many gardeners prefer them because they look nice and are supposedly easier to maintain because the crops are grown a foot or two higher than in ground rows which makes them easier to tend.

If you plan on spending hours picking out weeds one by one with your hands, then raised beds might be a good option for you. But I have no interest in performing time consuming tasks that could be completed much faster with a simple hand tool such as the hoe. You can't hoe raised garden beds unless you modify the angle of your hoe. But it's very easy to remove all the weeds with a hoe in an entire vegetable garden that's growing in the ground in under a hour.

Starting plants in raised beds is also supposedly easier than inground rows. Again this is true if you intend on raising or buying seedlings and then planting them out with your hands because there is less bending over. But I rarely grow crops from seedlings (we'll discuss why later), instead I sow them directly in the beds, something I can easily do standing up.

Raised beds have several other issues that few gardeners like to bring up. The soil in these gardens dries out twice as fast as in ground rows. This is because of the increased exposure to the wind and the nice looking boxes tend to heat up much faster than the ground.

Vegetables also do not like growing in raised beds because the beds restrict their roots *horizontally*. Most vegetables prefer to grow their roots out instead of down. That's because they are used to growing in the rich fluffy soils along rivers and there is no point establishing deep roots when all the nutrients are in the top few inches and your life cycle is less than a year.

When you grow vegetables in raised beds the roots are forced to compete more with each other instead of spreading out into the surrounding soil to collect water and nutrients. Raised beds are also more costly and require maintenance to keep them looking good, an extra expense that you can easily avoid by growing directly in the ground.

Further, the majority of garden tools are designed to be used with vegetables growing in the ground and not in raised beds. So unless you plan on climbing up onto your raised beds to work the soil, with your shovels, forks and hoes, you'll only have a small selection of inefficient hand tools available to maintain your crops.

Crops become much harder to maintain and harvest when they start growing from a 3 foot high raised garden bed and then reach 9-12 feet tall at the end of the season! So you'll either need to plant dwarf varieties of corn, tomatoes and other plants, which produce significantly lower yields, or you'll need to get a ladder and someone to hold it steady whilst you tend your crops.

Wind damage also increases when you grow your plants in raised garden beds. Not only do they lack the horizontal root systems to anchor themselves, but your crops are exposed to stronger winds than they are used to.

Raised beds are very inefficient to irrigate too. Irrigation nozzles have to be placed 3 feet taller than before which reduces the water pressure of existing systems and increases the number of sprinklers you'll need to cover the same area of garden. When your sprinklers are higher the water is exposed to stronger winds and more water will be lost to evaporation and wind drift.

You'll also need to bring in a significant amount of soil to fill your new garden beds. A bed that is 2 feet tall, 4 feet wide and 10 feet long will need 100 cubic feet of soil to fill it. Soil compacts as you fill your beds so even though the bed calculates at holding 80 cubic feet, you'll need to add an extra 20 cubic feet after the soil settles in the bed. Filling your raised garden beds with soil takes considerably more effort than double digging in ground garden beds.

Still, many gardeners prefer to grow in raised garden

beds. If that's you then that's OK, I'm not going to hold it against you. Just know that it is much harder to grow in raised beds than it is in the ground for all the reasons we've discussed above. Wherever possible grow your vegetables in the ground to save time, money and unnecessary effort.

Water: The Most Important Resource In Your Garden And How To Grow Plants Even In A Drought!

It was a cloudy day. The rain had poured down for most of the night and as I walked to Opa's house I had to side step puddle after puddle of water. Everywhere I looked was covered in soggy clay and pools of muddy water.

The only place that wasn't covered in water was Opa's vegetable garden. The soil there was wet to touch but not saturated like everywhere else. It looked as though the soil had just soaked up the rain like a big thirsty sponge.

"Don't step on the soil" Opa exclaimed as he handed me a hoe from his garden shed. He was carrying one too and had just finished sharpening the blades which were now as sharp as a razor. Closing the gate behind him he walked over to the first bed and started moving the hoe effortlessly through the bare dirt.

"When it rains the soil compacts. If it stays like this the sun will steal all the water out of our soil and then some!"

Opa moved the hoe back and forth between the crops swiftly, turning the compacted topsoil into a crumbly blanket that sat on top of the garden bed. After about 15 minutes we had hoed the entire vegetable plot. Hoeing the beds was easy. The hoes were sharp and the crops were spaced wide enough apart for the hoe to move between them.

I was curious if Opa did this every time he watered his garden. His response wasn't what I was expecting at all!

"I don't water my garden. The rain is all they need" he

responded, as he looked up at the cloudy sky happily.

"But you must water your plants during summer when there is no rain! How else will they survive?"

Chuckling lightly he nodded towards the garden bed in front of us

"Why did we just hoe the garden beds?"

"To keep the water in the soil..."

But surely the water wouldn't last the entire summer! The sun would just evaporate it and the rest would be used by the plants or leached away, right? That's what we're taught isn't it?

Opa knew differently. His father had taught him how they used to grow vegetables before irrigation existed and that's still how Opa tended his garden. He knew what most gardeners forget; soils are big sponges that soak up and hold onto a surprising amount of water. This is especially true for rich fertile loams like the soil in Opa had created in his vegetable garden.

There's also something that I learned much later when I was trying to figure how it was possible for soils to stay wet through summer without rain. All soils have capillary channels which suck moisture up out of the subsoil and into the topsoil to replace the moisture lost by transpiration and evaporation. But here's the thing, capillary action works best when the soil is already damp. If your soil dries out too quickly the capillary channels will break and the topsoil won't be able to draw up the moisture stored in the soil below.

The biggest draw down on the soils moisture levels is evaporation. When the soil is compacted it forms an unbroken capillary channel from the surface of the soil to the water stored in the subsoil. When the suns evaporation dries the surface of the soil, the soil continuously pulls moisture from below to try and keep the surface soil damp until finally the topsoil dries out and the capillary channel is broken.

Unfortunately by the time the capillary channel breaks the sun will have sucked your soil dry of all the available moisture. Your plants will be wilted and it'll be too late to do anything other than irrigate to save your crops.

When we hoe the top of the garden beds so the soil dries into a crumbly blanket across the top of our garden beds, we purposely break the capillary channel that connects our soil to the sun. By doing this we can keep significantly more moisture in the soil and reduce our soils evaporation levels to almost nothing. What's more, we strengthen the capillary channels that keep our topsoil moist because the sun is no longer drawing on the available moisture.

This is one of the reasons why regularly hoeing your garden beds is so important for vegetable gardens. It protects your soils from drying out too quickly and retains the maximum amount of water in the soil where it is available to your crops roots.

Almost all nutrients are water soluble as well. That means that without water, your crops can't access the nutrients in your soil. Too much water is also a bad thing as it can wash away nutrients and suffocate your plants roots.

The best watering system for all vegetable gardens imitates the rain. Infrequent deep watering will promote stronger plants that are more resistant to pests and diseases. Watering less often will also produce more concentrated flavors in your crops as it forces them to grow more roots in search of moisture. The more roots a plant grows the higher it's uptake of trace minerals, which are what gives our crops their unique flavors.

For areas with long dry summers you might want to install an overhead irrigation system to help keep your crops watered. Each time you water your garden either with a hose, irrigation or natural rain you should hoe the garden beds to keep the moisture locked into the soil. By doing this you can grow healthy vegetables even in the driest of summers with less than 1 watering per week.

This may sound extreme at first because so many vegetable gardeners are used to watering their gardens multiple times a day during the summer. But once you start hoeing the exposed soil regularly you'll reduce more than 80% of the water loss from your garden beds.

If you must apply additional water to your vegetable garden do so with overhead irrigation sprinklers early in the morning. The sprinklers should distribute water evenly over both garden beds *and paths*. If you only water the gardens the dry soil in the paths will suck the water right out of your beds. But when you water both the paths and beds you essentially double the stored water available in the soil for your crops.

Bare earth paths between the rows should also be hoed to form the crumbly blanket that protects the water from evaporating from the soil. It's important to water your gardens first thing in the morning so the soil has plenty of time to warm up before nightfall, which is when plants do the majority of their growing. Cold soil significantly reduces the growth and production of crops - another reason why over watering your garden can actually *reduce* your yields.

Why You Should Avoid Drip Irrigation

Drip irrigation systems have become extremely popular over recent years for backyard gardeners. Most gardeners are drawn to drip irrigation because these systems are more efficient at watering plants than overhead sprinklers.

Whilst it is true that drip irrigation has almost no

evaporation or wind drift loss, drip is not an efficient way to water your garden soil. The low application rate from the dripper nozzles means you'll have to run your irrigation for 5-10x longer than conventional overhead sprayers. This can increase the costs of watering your garden significantly.

The drip lines also make it very hard to hoe your garden beds, you'll either have to remove them when you work your gardens or move them out of your way as you tend to your crops. More often than not a misplaced hoe, spade or fork will puncture one of the many drip lines and you'll need to repair it. Whilst repairing drip lines is fairly simple, damaged pipe can go unnoticed for long periods of time and if left unrepaired the holes can suck dirt into the tubes and clog drippers downstream from the puncture.

Drip irrigation has many issues with supplying evenly to your crops. The area directly below the dripper gets the lion's share of the water, whilst the soil between drippers gets far less and can dry out rapidly. In sandy soils, where drip irrigation is most often used, the water quickly drains vertically through the soil rather than spreading out horizontally creating a very uneven water distribution.

Seeds which require a uniformly moist soil will not germinate well with drip irrigation and additional hand watering will be required. Seedlings also struggle with drip systems because much of the soil is left too dry whilst other parts become saturated and anaerobic, suffocating the growth of young roots.

Drip irrigation is very expensive too, a standard drip system requires running drip lines across your garden bed at 1 foot spacings so a 4 foot wide bed will have 4 drip lines running across it. For each system you'll also need a water filter, pressure reducer, flush and anti vacuum valves to ensure the drip lines work correctly.

As the drip lines heat up they tend to curl and twist, so

the perfect 1 foot wide spacings between lines can vary and change as much as 12 inches throughout the day. This creates a nightmare of uneven watering patterns especially if you're trying to start seeds or seedlings. Staking drip lines is pointless in our light and fluffy vegetable soils as the stakes do not stay in place.

The stakes and hoses are more an annoyance than anything and make it harder to hoe your beds. I recommend avoiding drip irrigation systems wherever possible. You'll be glad you did, overhead systems are much cheaper to install and maintain, plus they do a much better job at watering your crops!

How Often Should You Water?

Every garden is different. Some gardeners will never have to water their vegetable crops if they double dig their garden beds, improve the soil, have rainfall every 4-6 weeks and keep their soil regularly hoed.

Whilst other gardeners who live in places that have long dry summers or areas with less than 52 inches (1300 mm) of rain per year, will need to add some supplemental water to grow vegetable crops well. As a general rule vegetables will need 1 inch of water per week to produce a healthy harvest for mild climates, and an additional ½ inch for areas with very hot summers due to the increased transpiration from your crops.

If your area gets an annual rainfall of say 30 inches then you'll probably have to provide an additional 22 inches of water per year. You can do this at 1 inch per week, or several inches every few weeks which tends to grow stronger more tasty crops.

Sowing crops directly from seed instead of transplanting from seedlings will produce far stronger plants that need significantly less water and nutrients to grow. Transplanting seedlings creates significant stress on young plants It damages and stunts root development and reduces crop yields in the great majority of cases (tomatoes may be the only exception).

The best way to determine when your garden needs additional water is to check your soils moisture levels regularly. You can then adjust your irrigation system to water more often if your soil is too dry, or reduce the watering if it is too wet.

Over watering your garden will reduce the growth of your crops considerably. Every time you water you reduce the temperature of your soil by about half. Cooling your soil slows down the growth of your plants and ultimately reduces your yields. If you soil is constantly wet (because you irrigate too often) then there is less oxygen available to your plants roots which will stunt their growth and reduce yields also.

Soil that is depleted of oxygen is also low in microbes and it's the microbes that process the nutrients in the soil to feed your plants. Too much water will also increase the rate at which nutrients leach from your soil, which means you'll have to apply more fertilizers and amendments to keep crops growing.

As we discussed earlier, water also compacts the soil which increases the evaporation from your soil. So if you don't have time to hoe your garden soil a few hours after it's been watered you should avoid watering your garden because you'll end up with a *net loss* to the total amount of water in your soil.

Yes, your irrigation will add water to your garden and your crops will look like they have enough water, but if you don't hoe your soil the sun will suck your soil dry. It won't just suck up the water you've just applied but it'll also drain the reserves held in the subsoil too until all the moisture is gone and the capillary channel is broken by the dry soil.

This is why when gardeners water their vegetable gardens during the middle of a hot day there plants still continue to wilt even with the irrigation running. You can actually make your plants wilt by turning your irrigation on during the peak of the day as the sun will drain the water from your soil much faster than your sprinklers can put it out!

To determine the moisture level of your soil insert a shovel into the center of your garden bed lever to one side and then using your hand feel to see if the soil is cool and moist, or if it is dry. Ideally you should check the moisture level at least 3 inches below the surface of the garden bed. The top inch or two will always be a little drier than the rest.

If the soil at 6 inches deep is cool and moist then you do not need to water. If the soil is dry to touch then your plants could use a drink first thing tomorrow morning. You'd be surprised how many days your plants can grow on just the water reserves in the soil (yields won't decrease provided there is enough water in the soil, they'll tend to increase because crops will grow faster in the warmer ground).

One of the first things new seeds do is send a tap root 6-12 inches down into the soil to protect the seedling from extended periods of no rainfall. They do this *before* they send the stem up out of the soil and grow their first leaves. This is the natural instinct of all vegetables and one of the most important reasons why you should always sow seeds directly into garden beds instead of transplanting them.

Transplanted seedlings will wilt after just a few days without water because their tap root just grows around and around the seedling punnet instead of going deep into the soil. On the other hand, directly sown crops can go for 4-6 weeks very easily on the stored water in the soil when the soil is kept regularly hoed after rain. We'll talk more about plant spacing next, which is crucial to growing vegetables on low amounts of water and minimal fertilizers.

Growing Vegetables Even When There's No Water Supply

A hundred years ago if you wanted to grow vegetables and grains you had to do so from just the rainfall alone. There was no irrigation and bucketing water from the well or stream was a lot of work, especially when you've got acres of land to irrigate! Yet vegetable gardens thrived with nothing more than the natural rainfall of the area.

One of the reasons farmers could grow vegetables without water was that they used the correct plant spacings. Modern vegetable gardens try to cram far too many vegetables into a tiny space. Vegetables are not used to growing like this and their roots are forced to compete with each other for water and nutrients.

Closely planted vegetable gardens require daily or twice daily irrigation and extremely rich soils, with regular additions of fertilizers throughout the season. When plants are grown so closely together it's impossible to use a hoe to weed between them, which means you'll have to pull weeds and tend your gardens by hand!

Although the tight plant spacings may be good for gardeners with tiny plots, it requires far more water, fertilizer and maintenance to grow crops successfully. When vegetables are constantly competing with one another and force fed water and nutrients, they become very susceptible to pests and diseases. This is one of the reasons why so many backyard gardeners have such a problem with pests.

Intensive vegetable gardens such as the square foot garden or John Jeavons "intensive agriculture" make great use of small spaces, but at the cost of increased labor and resources. The yield per square foot may increase substantially, but if you've got the area to space your crops correctly, you can grow significantly more food with less resources over a wider area.

Correctly spacing your vegetable crops allows them to access water and nutrients without competing against each other. The paths between garden beds become valuable resources for plant roots too, greatly increasing the available water and nutrients to your crops.

Intensively planted gardens drain your soil of its moisture 20x faster than the sun's evaporation, creating a huge demand for additional irrigation and increasing the likelihood of nutrient toxicities building up in your soil.

Double digging garden beds increases the water holding capacity of the soil, which is why intensive vegetable gardens need to be double digged every single year. Whereas with wider spacing between plants, you will only need to double dig the soil once when you first prepare your garden. Each year thereafter you only need to turn the soil lightly with a fork to maintain the correct tilth.

By correctly spacing your plants you will grow bigger, pest resistant crops with far less effort, water and resources. Crops grown with sufficient spacing taste better and have greatly increased nutritional values as well.

Your free plant spacing chart that's included in this book is available at www.obsessedwithdirt.com/resources

The Secret To Perfect Soil

Opa had made a weird request the last time I saw him. He gave me an empty glass jar and told me to fill it with soil from my vegetable garden and bring it to him.

When I handed the jar to him he unscrewed the lid, shook half the dirt onto the ground, filled the jar with water and shook it vigorously before placing it down on the table in front of us.

Looking at the dirt in the jar he nodded his head as if to confirm something and then he turned to me with his cheeky smile and said

"This is no good"

Confirming my suspicions about my good-for-nothing dirt he sat back, watching patiently as more of the dirt settled out in the jar.

"Hmm..." he started as he leaned forward to look more closely at the jar full of dirt. I still had no idea what he was looking for or why we needed to do this before we could fix the soil in my garden. But I figured it was important, so I tried my best to understand what he was doing. Although at the time it felt like I was watching a witchdoctor as they read the future from my tea leaves...

"Your soil has lots of clay, plenty of silt but far too little sand" he said as he leaned back rocking in his chair happily.

"You see these layers here. They should all be mostly equal. The sand is the heaviest so it falls to the bottom almost immediately, then the clay which is lighter settles out on top and finally the silt which is the finest and lightest material rests gently here on the top"

I looked closely at the jar. There was ¼ of an inch of sand on the bottom, about 2 inches of clay and another inch of silt on the top. Opa sat back in his rocker and looked at me seriously, holding up three fingers as he began to speak

"After sunshine, plants need 3 things to grow well. Water, air and food. The sand keeps the soil open and full of air. The clay holds onto water and the silt feeds the roots. Plants must have all 3 or else they will not grow happily"

"But what about compost and manure? Don't plants need that too?"

"Yes, the silt is the compost and manure when it's broken down into food. But if there isn't enough sand in your soil your plants will suffocate. Not enough clay and your plants will always be thirsty. Too little silt and your plants will always be hungry"

I looked over to my jar of soil thinking about all the years I had spent trying to improve my soil by adding compost and manures. Why hadn't I read anywhere about adding sand to my heavy clay soils?

Opa's dirt-in-the-jar test was so simple and showed me exactly what I needed to add to my soil to fix it. I could test my soil every year easily and each year I could improve it by adding exactly what my soil needed so my plants could thrive.

Soils with the perfect balance of sand, silt and clay are called loams. They are exactly the type of soil you'll find along the floodplains of rivers that flood consistently every year and they are the best soil to grow vegetables in.

Most gardeners will be able to achieve a slightly sandy loam with just one addition of either locally sourced clay if your soil is naturally sandy, or course sand if you're growing in heavy clay. Once you've balanced your clay to sand ratio to roughly 50/50 then all you need to do each year is topdress your soil with an inch of compost to maintain and build a rich loam.

If your soil is too sandy it won't hold any water and will leach nutrients whenever it rains or is irrigated. Some sandy soils will even become hydrophobic and repel water due to a waxy film forming over each grain of sand. Adding organic matter to sandy soils only makes the soil dry out faster and repel more water. The hard grains of sand will grind the organic matter into a fine dust which will blow away with every gust of wind. It doesn't matter how often you water or fertilize sandy soils, they never hold onto the water or nutrients for long unless the soil contains clay.

The opposite is true for clay. These soils are hard to dig because they have too much clay and not enough sand. With the opposite effect of sandy ones, holding onto too much water and too much nutrients. Clay soils are notorious for poor drainage and nutrients can quickly build up to toxic levels and poison your crops. Gypsum will help open up clay soils and improve drainage *temporarily*, but the addition of course sand will permanently fix clay soils and transform them into a rich loam within a matter of weeks.

When you've got too much silt in your soil your plants will grow too quickly and become weak. Soils that are too rich have lots of pest and disease problems because the plants can't get enough calcium and magnesium which is held in the soil by clay and sand. Without calcium and magnesium your plants can't create strong cell walls to defend against pests and will even struggle to stand upright. Without sand the soil lacks structure and your plants roots won't be able to anchor to anything to protect themselves from the wind. Too little clay and all the silt quickly dries into a fine dust that doesn't hold together and instead blows away in the wind and runs off with each rainfall.

By now you should be able to see that soil needs to have all 3 of these key ingredients in equal quantities to grow healthy crops. Balancing sand, silt and clay is the most important and impactful thing you can do in your vegetable garden. It increases yields much more than fertilizing or watering your crops will.

The Dirt In The Jar Test

Testing your soil is easy and fun. I suggest you complete this exercise at the start of each growing season. You can then add a little sand, silt or clay to your soil before planting your crops and work your way to creating a rich loam.

There are a lot of gardening test kits on the market. All of them are a waste of money unless you've already balanced your soil. Getting the right soil consistency is far more important than having a pH between 5.5 and 7.5 or having high NPK levels.

Loam soils will naturally gravitate towards a slightly acidic pH around 6.5 which is what your plants prefer to grow in. Rich loam soils also hold onto a well balanced ratio of NPK as well as all the other macro and micronutrients, soil microbes and enzymes your crops need to thrive.

All you need for Opa's dirt-in-the-jar test is a mason jar, some water and a hand trowel.

1. Take a scoop of soil from the top foot of several of your vegetable garden beds
2. Mix the soil in a bucket until it is well combined, this will give you an average soil texture for the area tested
3. Fill the clear glass jar half way with the soil and then return the remaining soil to your garden
4. Add water to about ¾ full
5. Screw on the lid and shake vigorously for 1

minute
6. Set the jar down and leave it until the water turns clear which will take 1-3 days depending on your soil

Once the soil is settled in the jar you'll have 3-5 distinct layers in the jar. Starting from the bottom of the jar the layers will be:

1. Rocks and gravel
2. Sand
3. Clay
4. Silt
5. Uncomposted organic matter such as sticks, leaves and roots

Not all soils will have all 5 of these layers, but most soils will have varying levels of sand, silt and clay. Your goal is to have equal parts of sand, silt and clay in your soil which will create a rich dark loam that your vegetables will thrive in.

- If your soil is sandy add more clay. The best clay to use is Kaolin, however you can use any clay that is local to your area. Start with 55 pounds per 100 sq ft (25kg per 10m2)
- If your soil has too much clay add more sand. Make sure you choose pure sand as most builders sands are mixed with clay. Apply 6 inches of sand to your garden beds and mix in well with a garden fork
- If your soil has too much silt add more sand and clay, and stop adding compost and manures! Add 3 inches of a local soil that has roughly 50/50 sand and clay to your garden beds and mix in well

The best place to buy sand, silt or clay is at your local landscaping yard which will have plenty of different soils to choose from. You'll also be buying it in bulk directly from the supplier which will cost considerably less than buying it bagged or from a landscaper.

What About Compost And Manures?

Once you've balanced your gardens soil and created a loam, then you'll find that your soil needs far less amendments. A single application of 1 inch aged compost to your garden beds just before planting is all your soil needs to feed your crops and maintain tilth over the season.

Manures, although powerful fertilizers, are best avoided in the vegetable garden because they are too rich for most crops. The sudden dose of nitrogen produces splendid growth but also opens your plants up to being attacked by pests and diseases. Even aged manures can harbor large quantities of pests and diseases and are best added to your compost heap rather than directly to your garden beds.

In the old days when manure was one of the only fertilizers available, farmers added it to fields and then let it decompose for several weeks before they planted crops. The best way to add manures is to Opa's chicken tractor which we'll discuss in the next chapter.

Many gardeners make the mistake of thinking that they cannot add too much compost to the soil, but this isn't true. Even when your soil is a loam it can only hold onto a limited amount of organic matter and nutrients, the rest just leeches away and is lost forever. It is far better to apply a little compost often, than it is to apply a lot of compost all at once.

Gardens that have been overfed with compost grow plants that are weak and susceptible to pests and diseases. Plants need a balanced diet of all the macro and micro nutrients, not just the ones found in compost. Many of the most important nutrients such as calcium, magnesium and silica come from the sand, stones and clay in the soil and are not readily available in compost.

Making compost the way the gardening magazines teach is both wasteful and time consuming. I don't know about you but I can't be bothered turning the compost heap, watering and carefully monitoring it every few days to make good compost. Whenever I've tried making compost in heaps or with tumblers it's never worked out. More often than not I just end up wasting my time trying to make compost when I could be enjoying my garden instead.

Compost heaps are also terribly inefficient at capturing and storing nutrients, which is why most homemade composts low in nutrients. Most of the nutrients end up leaching into the soil *beneath* the compost heap instead of actually staying in the compost itself!

If you don't have room or time to make your own compost then you can buy well aged commercial compost from the landscape yard. Old mushroom compost is usually the highest quality and is made from equal parts cow manure and lucerne straw. You might even get some edible mushrooms growing in your garden!

The Lazy Gardeners Method To Make Rich Compost From Practically Anything

It was time to pull out the cabbages growing in the bed. They had thrived over the winter months, producing huge tasty heads and their leaves spread out in circles 3 feet wide. I had never seen cabbage plants this big before.

Pulling them out was harder than I had anticipated too. Each plant had massive roots that grew up to 10 feet in every direction. They were no match for Opa though, with his handheld machete he effortlessly chopped his way around the plant and threw it up into the wheelbarrow beside us.

In the end I let him chop and pull up the cabbages and I stacked them on the main path. After a few minutes Opa had pulled the entire bed and there was now a gigantic pile of green cabbage plants on the path next to us. Opa threw two more of them into the wheelbarrow and headed off down the path.

"But what about the roots left in the garden?" I asked.

"Food for our friend the worm" he replied, as he set the wheelbarrow down in front of him. The garden bed in front of us had a large mesh box sitting over it. The box was exactly the size of the bed and had a hinged lid on top. Opa grabbed his machete and chopped everything in the wheelbarrow into small pieces then opened the lid on the mesh box and dumped everything inside.

"Now all we need is my compost activator" he said with a chuckle as he strode proudly off to the shed at the end of the garden. He returned with a big hessian sack, emptied it into the box and closed the lid standing back proudly.

"Ta da"

"Chickens?"

"These girls make the best compost. They turn the pile every day. Eat all the bugs. Add manure and make eggs too. I put all the garden waste and kitchen scraps in here and they turn it into compost. Plus they even spread it all over the garden bed for me!"

"After a few weeks I'll move them to another bed where they'll eat all the bugs and leftover seeds, turn the soil and make more compost for me"

I stood back appreciating Opa's clever little composting system. The chickens happily pecked and scratched through the soil eating the bugs and cabbage leaves. This really was the easiest way to make compost.

All Opa had to do was throw in the garden scraps and the chickens would do the rest. There was no turning piles or carting compost around the garden. Best of all, all the nutrients went straight into the garden bed rather than leeching away under the compost heap.

The mesh box, which Opa nicknamed as his "Chicken Tractor", was light enough that it could be picked up by two people and moved easily from one bed to the next. Opa had even added some wheels so he could move it by himself whenever he wanted to.

Having the chicken tractor saved Opa from doing most of the backbreaking work in his garden. About the only thing difficult about it was moving it from one bed to another, but even that was surprisingly easy.

The tractor fit perfectly over the garden bed and could house up to four chickens comfortably. You don't need to buy any chicken feed because all the food comes from the the kitchen scraps and wastes from your garden.

All the worms and bugs provided a very high protein feed for the chickens too. They worked hard scratching through the soil to find every bug and worm they could find. After all the scratching and digging the chickens would leave the soil fluffy and crumbly. They will eat and break down everything in the topsoil into a rich compost within just a few weeks.

When the chickens have finished working the soil it is absolutely perfect for sowing seeds. There's plenty of manure and compost spread around, all the bugs and seeds are gone and it's a perfect tilth.

I recommend clearing a garden bed of the crops first and then letting the worms come in and eat all the leftover roots for a week. This way when you add the chicken tractor the chickens get a nice treat of worms in the first few days. You can leave the chickens in the tractor to work the soil for anywhere from a few days to several months.

As long as you're always adding new organic matter into the coop you can leave the chicken tractor on the same bed for as long as you like. Just keep in mind that it is possible to over fertilize a garden bed. Generally I've found that 2-4 weeks is the perfect length of time for the chickens to work the soil.

When you're just starting your garden, or if your next crop is especially hungry (like cabbages) then you can add manure to the chicken tractor to boost the soils fertility. The chickens will work the manure into the soil and also eat any pests or bugs that are hidden in it.

If you're just establishing your garden then I'd also recommend keeping a mineral block in the chicken tractor too. This is a great way to correct and balance your soils minerals. If the garden waste that you're feeding your chickens is missing a certain nutrient then the chickens will peck mostly that nutrient out of the mineral block and then add it to your soil via their manure.

Mineral blocks can be bought very cheaply from farm supply stores and are all natural products. You'll have significantly healthier chickens and crops after just a few months of adding the mineral block to your chicken tractor. Plus you'll get far better tasting eggs and poultry!

The best poultry breeds for chicken tractors are the larger dual-purpose breeds because they find it harder to dig out of the enclosure and escape. Although if you keep your chickens well fed you won't have them escaping anyway! You'll also find that as they scratch the soil, the dirt tends to mound up around the perimeter of the enclosure which reduces their escape tendencies.

These are the chicken breeds I highly recommend:

- Black Australorp
- Rhode Island Red
- Orpington

You can download the free plans for the chicken tractor and other resources included in this book by going to www.obsessedwithdirt.com/resources

Should You Keep Your Soil Covered?

When it comes to growing vegetables the answer is clear, absolutely not. Covering your soil with mulches such as straw or other types of organic matter cools the soil down. Vegetables do not like to grow in soil that is too cool and will have much lower yields and slower growth overall.

Mulched garden beds also make it nearly impossible to sow seeds directly into the soil. First the soil is usually too cold to germinate the seeds, so it must be raked away, and secondly mulched soils hold too much water which tends to rot the seeds before they germinate.

Many gardeners think that exposed soil has high evaporation rates and so it must always be covered in mulch. Whilst this is partially true for compacted soil, the crumbly soil from regularly hoed garden beds has almost no evaporation. By hoeing your soil after rain or irrigation you reduce the evaporation rates by more than 80%.

Mulches also have a bad habit of holding onto and absorbing water. Wet and soggy mulches will rot the stems of your crops and increase the spread of diseases in the garden. Pests also find safety under the cover of mulch and are much harder to keep under control in mulched beds.

As mulches break down they take up a draw nitrogen from your soil to turn break down the carbon in the organic matter. When bacteria and fungi are encouraged to break down mulches they temporarily reduce the available nitrogen in your soil, until the mulch has been broken down. If your beds are always mulched then the nitrogen is always being used to break down the mulches and never returned to the soil.

Vegetables thrive in a bacteria dominated soil and when you keep your soil covered in mulch you encourage fungi to take over in your soil. Vegetable crops don't like to grow in fungi dominated soils and will be more susceptible to pests and diseases, slower to grow and have reduced yields.

Trying to weed a mulched garden bed is impossible to do with a hoe, which means you'll have to hand weed instead. The reason why mulched garden beds have fewer weeds than bare earth beds is that the soil never heats up enough to germinate the weed seeds. So whenever you remove the mulch from the bed the patiently waiting weed seeds quickly germinate in retaliation! Making it frustratingly impossible to germinate seeds in mulched rows.

However, there are some acceptable times that you should mulch your garden beds. Perennial crops such as asparagus, artichoke, rhubarb and berries, prefer to grow in cooler soils and will thrive when their beds are kept mulched.

If you live in an area with very cold winters then you might also want to cover your garden beds with mulch to keep your soil warmer through winter. This will help you plant out your garden earlier in spring and it helps protect your soil bacteria through the cold.

I also strongly suggest using mulch on other parts of your garden such as your orchard, shrubs and any perennial garden beds. Keeping your perennial gardens mulched is a great way to protect them from droughts, reduce the spread of weeds and *slowly* feed your soil with nutrients as the mulch breaks down.

Stop Wasting Money On Expensive Fertilizer and Make Your Own All Natural Fertilizer For 1/10th The Price

"What's that you're spreading on the dirt Opa?

"Just a little bit of magic" he said with a coy smile as he continued spreading the mixture in a bed of corn that was already well over 12 feet tall and growing rapidly. Each stem had a heavy cob filled with fat rainbow colored kernels, an old heirloom variety Opa had been growing for years called *Glass Gem*.

I looked into the bucket at the strange mixture trying to figure out what he was feeding the corn to get it to grow so quickly. It looked nothing like the fertilizers sold at the store, instead Opa's fertilizer was a course and a blended brown in color.

"Do you remember where vegetables grow?" Opa asked, sifting his hands through his bucket of homemade fertilizer.

"Along the floodplains of the river" I replied

"Good. Now when the river floods many things happen."

"The water flows quickly picking up debris and rocks and grinding everything into dust. When the river reaches the floodplains, which are wide and flat, the water slows down and everything that was ground up settles onto the floodplains.

"This is how the rich fertilizers the soil for the vegetables to grow"

Opa had an inspired look on his face as he handed me

the bucket and walked into his garden shed. Inside there was a small bench, half a dozen tools with long handles and a few large sacks stacked in the corner.

He scooped from the first sack pouring a handful of what looked like breadcrumbs into the bucket. He reached into another sack and added a fine white powder to my bucket, and then continued to add a little from each sack before stirring it all together in the bucket.

"Crushed plants, ground rocks, bones, and ash from the fire, that's what the river deposits on the floodplains to enrich the soil."

Opa's fertilizer was so simple to make. He bought everything in big sacks and then mixed it together as he used it. All the ingredients were easy to find and incredibly cheap too, making Opa's fertilizer worked out to be almost 1/10th the price of the fertilizers in the store.

It's unbelievable what fertilizer companies can get away with. When tested most commercial fertilizers are stuffed with industrial waste products, high in heavy metals and other toxic substances that kill soil life and can build up to toxic levels in your garden.

So it's no wonder plants become sick and malnourished when all they have to grow with is chemicals and dead dirt. There are some gardeners who swear by these toxic fertilizers and proudly present their picture perfect vegetables in defense of their chemical addiction.

When you test these vegetables at the agricultural laboratory they have less than half the nutrients of organically grown crops. What's more, they cost a small fortune in fertilizers and pesticides to produce. No thank you!

The DIY All Natural Fertilizer That Will Revolutionize Your Vegetable Garden

You can make up a big batch of this fertilizer and store it, or make it as you use it like Opa did. It'll last indefinitely when stored in an airtight container and kept dry. The recipe is Opa's complete organic fertilizer, so you won't need to apply anything else to grow crops that thrive and produce big yields of delicious vegetables.

Apply 4-6 quarts per 100 square feet to your garden beds at the start of the growing season and rake loosely into the top inch of the soil before you sow your seeds. Then reapply 1 quart per 100 square feet every 6 weeks for hungry feeders like tomatoes, corn and most fruiting plants.

Don't use this on root crops, as most will grow better if you *don't* fertilize them. There will be plenty of leftover nutrients in the soil from last years crops for these plants to feed on, and by not fertilizing you'll encourage root crops to grow bigger roots as they search for food.

Opa's Complete Organic Fertilizer Recipe

Mix uniformly, in parts by volume:

- 4 parts of any seed meal such as Neem, Alfalfa, Soy
- 1/4 part ordinary agricultural lime, best finely ground
- 1/4 part gypsum
- 1/2 part dolomite lime
- 1 part bone meal, rock phosphate or high-phosphate guano
- 1 part kelp meal or basalt dust
- 1 part charged biochar

You can download this fertilizer recipe and a list of resources for sourcing these ingredients from

Feeding Your Crops With Seed Meals

Plants put a lot of energy into producing seeds for the next season which is why ground up seeds make such a great fertilizer. Seed meal is high in nitrogen, minerals and potassium which makes it a great all round feed that you can use in any garden. Being a byproduct of the oil manufacturing industry seed meal is cheap and readily available too.

The only downside to using seed meal as a fertilizer is that some seeds are grown from GMO crops and heavily sprayed with chemicals. Luckily the majority of these chemicals have to be removed prior to the seeds being processed into consumer grade oils, so only a fraction of the chemicals remain on the processed seed meal. But to be safe I prefer to use only non-GMO seeds which are usually sprayed with far fewer chemicals when they are grown.

Nitrogen, Potassium and Phosphorus amounts vary greatly depending on the different seeds being used in the meal. Generally seed meals with high protein content will have equally high concentrations of NPK, whereas low protein seeds will have lower NPK values. Here are the most common seed meals with their protein and NPK ratios:

- Neem - 34% protein with an NPK of 6-1-2 (my preferred seed meal)
- Alfalfa - 17% with 2-1-2
- Soy - 36% with 7-2-1
- Cotton - 33% with 5-2-1

You can find many different seed meals for cheap prices at livestock and farm supply stores, where they are sold as a livestock feed replacement. Seed meals are popular among farmers because the high carbohydrate content can quickly fatten an animal in the final weeks before they send it to slaughter.

Protecting Your Plants With Lime

Regularly adding lime to your garden soils is easily the single most important thing you can do to grow better vegetables. Adding lime to to your soil will help your plants grow big and strong. Calcium, which is the main component in most limes, will ensure your plants grow strong cell walls, enabling them to fight off pests and diseases easily.

Even if your garden soil is alkaline, the addition of the small amount of lime in this fertilizer will not increase the pH of your soil, *unless* it is below 6.0. The pH scale is *not* a linear measurement from 1-14 like many people think, instead it is a logarithmic scale where each number is 10 times greater than the last. So a pH of 6 is 10 times more acidic than a pH of 7, and 100 times more acidic than a pH of 8.

Increasing your soils pH with the addition of lime is easy in acidic soils that have a pH of less than 6.0, but the higher the pH the less effect lime has on the soil. High pH soils generally have a high level of calcium, but this calcium is locked up in unavailable forms which is why you still need to apply lime to even alkaline soils.

If you plan on using a chicken tractor or spreading compost over your beds then this will tend to make your soil more acidic over time. Vegetables like to grow in a soil with a pH between 6 and 6.5, anything below 5 or above 7 tends to reduce the growth and yields of most vegetable crops.

Many gardeners fuss over pH far too much. Focus on balancing your soils sand, clay and silt to achieve a loam and your soil will naturally balance itself to a pH of 6-6.5. Loam soils are fantastic regulators of soil pH, nutrients and water, which is why they are the most first crucial step to growing a better vegetable garden.

Agricultural lime helps helps plants build strong cell walls to protect themselves from pests because it is high in absorbable calcium. Healthy plants require a surprisingly large amount of calcium to grow, only nitrogen and potassium are used in larger amounts by plants.

Once the plant has absorbed calcium from the soil and used it to build cell walls in the leaves, stems and fruits, the calcium becomes fixed and cannot be redistributed around the plant. This is why you'll often see pests attacking the new growth instead of the old, because your plant has run out of calcium in the soil and can no longer build strong cell walls to defend against attacks.

It's important to use *both* agricultural lime and dolomite lime because dolomite lime also has magnesium. Plants use a lot of magnesium during photosynthesis. Without magnesium the chlorophyll in your plants leaves cannot capture the sun's energy and photosynthesis doesn't happen which can quickly starve your plants of the sun's energy.

Soils that are sandy or acidic tend to leech magnesium quickly. Plants that are magnesium deficient have tell-tale yellow leaves with green veins. Dolomite lime has caught a bad rap recently because some gardeners have mistaken it for agricultural lime and applied far too much dolomite to their soils which can create a magnesium toxicity. Too much magnesium shows as a brown burning around the leaves edges and stunts plant growth.

The ratios used in the homemade fertilizer are well balanced and won't lead to any toxicity or deficiencies in your soil. Correcting your soil to a loam will also protect you from any nutrient imbalances.

Keeping Your Soil Light And Fluffy With Gypsum

Another rich calcium source, gypsum is essential for keeping your soil light and fluffy. It is especially useful for opening up heavy clay based soils making them much easier to dig. Many gardeners ignore gypsum thinking that it is just used to break up clay soils, but gypsum also adds two important nutrients to your garden - calcium and sulphur.

We've already discussed many of the benefits of adding calcium to your soil but sulphur is just as important. If you were to place all the nutrients in order of importance for plant health, sulphur would by 9th and calcium 7th.

One of the key benefits of sulphur is its ability to regulate the sodium in the soil. If your soil has too much sodium then the calcium becomes unavailable to your plants - no matter how much calcium you add to your soil!

Unlike agricultural and dolomite limes which do not dissolve into the soil and must be dug in to have any effect, the calcium in gypsum is water soluble and immediately available to plant roots. In soils with a pH higher than 7, much of the calcium in dolomite and aglime can't be accessed by plants, which is why even in alkaline soils plants can become calcium deficient.

The reason gypsum loosens up compacted soils is because the sulphur leeches excess sodium from the soil and replaces it with calcium. Plant roots are slower to grow in compacted soils not because of the smaller pore space, but because compacted soils have too much sodium and excess sodium burns and discourages root development.

Gypsum also helps organic matter and nutrients move

through soils, which is why gypsum treated soils have a deeper topsoil than soils were no gypsum has been applied. In short, if you want to create well balanced deep black soils then you need to apply gypsum to your garden beds regularly.

Rock Phosphate Grows Stronger Roots

Phosphorus has a terrible tendency to leech from even the best of soils. It is particularly difficult to keep phosphorus in sandy soils.

Phosphorus helps plants convert other nutrients into building blocks that they can use to grow. Without phosphorus your plants will be stunted, produce very low yields and weak root systems. There is little risk of applying too much phosphorus to your soil because phosphorus leeches away so quickly and is difficult for your plants to absorb.

Rock phosphate is a great source because it has the most available phosphorus of all phosphate fertilizers. I prefer to use a 50/50 blend of rock phosphate and bone meal which releases the nutrient slowly as the soil microbes process the bone dust. This creates a well rounded and consistent supply of phosphorus over 1-2 months.

Most bone meals are made from cow bones and provide both nitrogen and phosphorus to your garden with an NPK of 3-15-0. Whilst rock phosphate generally has a lower phosphorus level of 0-5-0 and a slower release of nutrients.

Kelp Meal Is The Secret To Tasty Vegetables

If you want to grow tastier vegetables that are full of nutrients and popping with vibrant colors then you need to apply kelp meal. Kelp is dried seaweed and rich in trace minerals. This fast growing seaweed can grow as much as 3 feet a day in the ocean making it a renewable and ample source of minerals for your garden.

There are over 70 natural vitamins and minerals in kelp that help you grow stronger plants with richer flavors and brighter colors. When added to the soil kelp will take about 4 months to release all of its nutrients which makes it a great slow release fertilizer. Soil microbes, bacteria and fungi thrive on the rich array of nutrients found in kelp, giving your plants yet another boost to their health and flavor.

Kelp meal has an NPK of 1-0-4 which complements the seed meal and phosphorus fertilizers perfectly, creating a balanced fertilizer with an NPK of 10-10-6

Biochar Supercharges Everything In Your Garden

Biochar is wood that has been turned into charcoal and is largely resistant to decomposition. It significantly enhances the nutrient and water retention of your soil helping to capture and store more nutrients for your plants to use.

When used in the garden biochar will double the nutrient and water holding capacity of regular soils, and can triple the storage in loams. Soils that are regularly amended with biochar will develop deeper and richer topsoils.

It's important to only use 'charged' biochar in your vegetable garden because uncharged biochar will have a temporary drawdown of nutrients from the surrounding soil. The nutrients will become available again after a few days, but it can temporarily stunt the growth of your crops.

Charged biochar has been soaked in a nutrient rich liquid to 'charge' the millions of pores with nutrients so it doesn't have any drawdown when added to garden soils.

Biochar readily exchanges these nutrients

It also helps regulate soil ph, reduces heavy metal toxicity, boosts beneficial bacteria and fungi.

How To Make Vegetable Gardening Effortless and Eliminate BackBreaking Work With These 7 Essential Tools

Opa was well into his 90's when he taught me about growing vegetables, yet he had no trouble maintaining his 4000 square foot garden. He never used any tractors or powered equipment, instead relying on less than a dozen hand tools to work his soil and tend his crops.

The tools were one of the only possessions he brought with him when he migrated from Holland 70 years ago. They had served him well, helping him feed his family in good times and bad. Each tool was exceptionally maintained with classic wooden handles and sharp edges on clean rust free steel.

"Where are the rest of your tools Opa?" I asked, in disbelief that anyone, even a gardener as skilled as him, could maintain a vegetable plot this big with just a few basic hand tools.

"I am old. Why spend all day working the soil when the work is already being done by someone else?"

"After the soil is fixed there is little left to be done. The worms will turn the soil and keep it open for the plants roots to grow. Whilst I get my chickens to prepare new beds, working in the compost, apply manure and eat all the bad bugs, seeds and weeds"

"All the hard work is done for me. I only need to rake the soil to sow the seed and then hoe the beds after it rains to keep the water in. Everything else is done for me and all that's left is to harvest what grows"

Think about all the modern inventions used in the

vegetable garden that only end up creating more work for the you. Rotary tillers with their fast moving blades, destroy all the worms and soil life as the machine fluffs up the soil. They leave the soil compacted, dry and lifeless with every pass of the blades. Compost bins need turning, worm farms need emptying and tools with movable parts are always breaking and need repairing.

But could I really grow a vegetable garden with just 7 tools?

I already had many similar tools to Opa's essential 7, but the handles were always breaking, blades were dull and the steel was covered in rust. Years ago I bought myself a bunch of cheap gardening tools naively thinking that my petrol powered machines would do all the hard work for me.

Instead I found myself relying on my hand tools far more than I had anticipated. The machines could only work part of the soil and left a lot of work to be done by hand. Every time I used my cheap tools the poor designs and low quality manufacturing worked against every movement.

Trying to use these tools made my back ache like crazy and gave my hands blisters. The blades were blunt but I never thought to sharpen them, which meant I had to drive the blades into the dirt with all my might to cut through anything. Handles regularly snapped from the impact of blunt tools hitting hard ground.

I remember the first time I used one of Opa's tools because it was such a major contrast to what I was used to. The sharp edges effortlessly glided through all the roots and dirt. I needed to exert almost no effort to work the soil. Each tool had a long strong handle that eliminated any bending or straining movements making it incredibly easy to work the soil whilst standing upright.

Sadly the brilliant company who made Opa's tools was

long gone. High quality garden tools used to be a necessity for every gardener but have recently been replaced with cheap fakes. Manufacturers are deliberately producing tools that are difficult and costly to repair. Instead they want you to keep coming back and buying new tools year after year. Finding well made tools for your vegetable garden isn't as easy as it should be.

If you want a list of the tools I recommend and a link to their suppliers then download the free book resources from www.obsessedwithdirt.com/resources

Vegetable Garden Snips

Opa had originally brought with him a heavy pair of gardening secateurs from Holland, but after years of sharpening the blade finally wore out. They did last him a good 10 years daily use but without a replacement blade available he had to find a new pair.

Over the years he has tried many different garden secateurs, shears and snips. There is one lightweight pair of well made garden snips that is highly recommends. Unlike secateurs which are designed for pruning woody plants, garden snips have a small pointed blade that is perfect for getting into tight areas. This is great when you need to harvest tomatoes, beans and other fruits from your crops..

Garden snips are easily the most essential gardening tool in your shed. You'll carry them with you everywhere you go. A good pair of snips is spring loaded, lightweight and durable. They should fit comfortably in your hand and be easy to take apart and sharpen.

Replaceable blades and springs should be available in case you need to make some simple repairs. Although my preference is to just buy a new pair once every few years when the blade begins to wear down because these days it's cheaper to buy a new pair than pay for the shipping on the replacement parts.

When I buy the snip online I'll also buy a few extra blades and springs at the same time. By doing this I'll only pay for shipping once and when the tool breaks I've already got the spare parts on hand in the shed - just remember where you put them!

Hori Hori

The Hori Hori is always secured to Opa's belt. I don't think I've ever seen him in the garden without this tool nearby and for good reason too, because it is incredibly useful. The Hori Hori can help you do practically anything in your garden including weeding, digging, measuring, pruning, cutting and harvesting crops.

When looking for a Hori Hori always buy one with a well made sheath to store the tool in. Not only is it easier to loop this tool to your belt, but the blades are dangerously sharp and the sheath protects you from any accidental cuts. For a well made and long lasting tool look for a Hori Hori with a full tang through the handle which will give the tool extra strength.

The Hori Hori is great for cutting through anything that is too thick or tough for the garden snips to handle. I use it to harvest pumpkins and chop up plants before adding them to the chicken tractor.

One of the things I love most about my Hori Hori is the handy measuring marks on the blade. I find myself using it often to measure fruits and check the depth of seed furrows before I sow. The ruler is also useful when you're thinning out seeds to the correct spacings in the bed.

Ergonomic Shovel

You've probably already got a shovel in your shed so you might be tempted to skip over this tool but don't! I was given one of these 'ergonomic' tools as a gift and it sat in my shed for years until I finally gave up repairing my cheap shovel.

I still remember the first hole I dug with the ergonomic shovel. It was the easiest hole I have ever dug! No sore back, and it took considerably less effort to move the dirt around. If you do a lot of digging, then getting an ergonomic shovel like this one is an absolute must!

It's an absolute lifesaver when it comes to double digging new garden beds or planting out a new orchard. The smaller head on this shovel is great for getting into tight spaces and digging out old crops or transplanting. With a slightly curved head it's also very handy for shoveling dirt or compost around the yard.

Bow Rake

Getting the right tilth is essential for germinating seeds. Garden beds need to be regularly raked free of debris and should be levelled before sowing seeds. A good quality bow rake will help you prepare your beds, spread manures and composts, and cleanup after your crops have been harvested.

The best bow rakes for backyard gardeners are lightweight, durable and have heads made of good quality steel. You'll find many cheaper rakes only secure the handle to the centre of the head and this is a very weak design. Good quality bow rakes should always connect the handle to both ends of the head which helps distribute the load evenly and greatly reduces strain and snapped handles.

Bow rakes are usually a one time only purchase and will last you for 50 or more years of regular use. So it makes sense to invest in a well made tool that you can rely on for the long term, instead of just a cheap knock off.

Garden Fork

Garden forks are essential for turning compost heaps, uprooting large plants and preparing new garden beds. Forking over a garden bed is one of the most labor intensive tasks in the vegetable garden. Having an ergonomic garden fork makes breaking open new ground considerably easier and reduces both the strain and effort involved.

Look for a garden fork with a radial handle which is far more comfortable than the standard D handle type. Choosing a fork with a resin encased steel shaft keeps the tool lightweight and is nearly impossible to break. A good quality garden fork will see you through decades of regular use and save hours of backbreaking work. Nothing is more frustrating to use than a weak garden fork that snaps or bends when you try to work the soil!

Yard Cart

Opa had made himself several wooden yard carts over the years. For most gardeners going to that effort isn't worthwhile. Today there's many well designed and very useful yard carts available online.

My favorite yard cart is the Aerocart. I have to admit that the first time I saw it I thought it was pretty ridiculous. It's at least 4 different carts combined into one, and makes working in your vegetable garden so much easier.

There's a sling to lift up and transport heavy rocks and planters easily. The wheelbarrow is a great size and very durable and the kickshoe doubles as a bench when it is folded flat and a fridge trolley when it is down.

I found that the weight distribution was incredibly well managed in the Aerocart. It doesn't matter how light or heavy the load is, or where you've positioned it. Having two wheels on the yard cart instead of one ensures the weight is evenly distributed and the cart is easy to maneuver.

Action Hoe

There are a lot of different types of garden hoes available but Opa found that he only really needed one - the action hoe. If you want to quickly weed a garden bed then the fast action hula hoe is exactly what you need. Just glide the hula back and forth through your soil and it will cut the weeds from their roots killing them in one quick motion.

You can easily remove the weeds with a bow rake or the back of the hoe after you've finished weeding. The action hoe is essential for large vegetable gardens and for gardeners who want to avoid bending over to weed beds (ahem, everyone).

Keep the front and back blades of this hoe sharp so you can make use of both the forward and back strokes for maximum efficiency. It's common to see some gardeners complaining about hoes not cutting through weeds easily and that's because they don't sharpen their hoe. Keep a sharp edge and your hoe will slice through even the thickest of weed roots with ease.

You can download the free essential tools list and a list of suppliers that stock them from www.obsessedwithdirt.com/resources

The One Tool Almost Every Gardener Never Uses That Would Make Working In Your Garden 100x Easier

The most important tool you could own is not even used in the garden. It's used on the blades of your gardening tools to keep them sharp. Trying to garden with blunt tools is the most frustrating thing you could possibly do.

Even a brand new tool purchased at the store will have a dull edge. Manufacturers rarely sharpen their tools until sharp because the sharpened edge is easily damaged during transit, the blades pose a greater safety risk to workers and increased liability from consumers.

Sharpening the blades also adds additional cost to the manufacturing process. Not to mention that the majority of consumers wouldn't be able to tell the difference between a sharp tool and a blunt one until they've used it. At which point, they've already purchased the tool and the manufacturer has made their money.

Most gardeners have never even felt the difference that a sharp tool can make to routine gardening tasks. Simple things such as digging a hole, forking over new ground or hoeing weeds from garden beds are all made much easier with a tool that has a sharp edge.

Dull tools cause more injury than sharp ones too because they require significantly more strain and force to achieve the same task. Instead of a sharp shovel cutting through plant roots in one motion, blunt shovels require you to rip or tear roots using repetitive force.

Fortunately, learning to select tools with the right steel hardness and how to sharpen them is easy. The time it takes to keep your tools sharp is quickly rewarded with reduced efforts and more ease-of-use when you're working your soil so make sure you keep tools sharp!

Hard vs Soft Steel, Which Is Better?

Not all tools are created equally. Some will bend, snap or crack after just a few hours of moderate use, whilst others go on to last multiple decades. So what sets good tools apart from the ordinary?

Aside from being well designed, your tool needs to be made of the right grade of steel. Metals are unique in that they can be smelted together with other metals and materials to form alloys with a wide range of applications from heavy steel beams to aluminum foil.

Garden tools are made from steel with a wide range in hardness levels. Hard steel is harder to sharpen but will hold the edge for a long time before it needs to be sharpened again. It is also much more likely to crack or snap from being impacted against something hard. Tools such as secateurs, snips, hedge shears and knives are best made from hard steel, so the blades stay sharp through repeated use.

Soft steel has its place in the garden too. It is the best steel to use for tools where brute force impacts are likely to happen. The soft steel tends to 'bounce' and flex *instead of snapping* when it hits another dense object. This is the type of steel used in garden axes (very soft steel), shovels, hoes and forks. The tradeoff however is that the softer the steel is the faster it loses its sharpened edge.

Axes which have the softest steel should be sharpened before each use to get the best efficiency and longest life. Whereas shovels, hoes and forks are usually made of semi-hard steel and will hold an edge from a few days to several months depending on how much you use them.

This isn't to say that all shovels are made from soft steel and all secateurs from hard steel though. Soft steel is cheaper to manufacture and many tools makers in search of higher profit margins make all their tools with cheap soft steel.

There is also cheap hard steel because it isn't tempered correctly, and some manufactures use this steel in their tools as well. Steel that hasn't been tempered correctly is very brittle and these are the shovels that snap or crack easily when you hit a stone in the dirt.

It's important that you know how to tell the difference between soft and hard steels to choose the best quality tools. Testing the hardness of steel is very easy, and can be done with a metal file and a little elbow grease.

Soft steel easily and quickly files away whereas hard steel takes much longer to sharpen. The easiest way to compare tools is to take your file with you to the store and run a few strokes across the blade of the tools you want to compare. Keep the angle and pressure consistent and after about 10 strokes per tool you'll know for sure what grade of steel was used in each tool.

Should all your tools be made of hard steel or soft steel? The answer depends on your garden and not on any one preference. If you're gardening in soil that has a lot of rocks and big tree roots then you should choose tools with softer steel because they are more tolerant of being knocked around.

For all cutting tools such as knives and secateurs try to find the hardest steel possible so you don't have to sharpen these blades as often. And if your garden has soil that is very light (sandy soils) with very few rocks, then you can confidently choose hard steel for your shovels too.

How To Sharpen Your Tools Correctly

The first time you sharpen a brand new tool from the store is always the hardest. Most tools will come completely unhoned which means the steel is cut at a square 90 degree angle on all sides. Grinding this down to a blade with an angle of 15 degrees will take quite a long time to do. Once it's done however, maintaining the edge is as easy as a few strokes with your file once a month.

First you'll want to make sure you're using a steel file that is in good condition. If your file is rusty, dirty or dull then you need to throw it out and get a new one. You can pick up a new steel file for a couple of bucks at any hardware store. They only last a few years if you're using them regularly and it pays to replace them when they get damaged or worn.

Start by rubbing some oil into the grooves of your file. This will help keep the metal grindings out of the valleys and also lubricate the surface of the file to make filing easier. If you've used your file previously then use a stiff metal brush to remove any dust, dirt or metal shavings from the valleys before you oil and use it.

To sharpen a shovel, place it on the edge of a porch or on the ground and hold it firmly with your foot. You can also get someone else to hold it whilst you sharpen the edge if this is easier, or secure it in a bench vice which is what I usually do. Use a protractor (yes you need to be precise!) to position the file at a 15 degree angle and stroke the file along the edge of the blade firmly.

You should try to only file your tool on the downward stroke (push stroke) and release pressure on the upward stroke. This will help you maintain a consistent angle as you file your tool which creates a sharper and longer lasting edge.

For the best results you should move your file across the whole blade in one smooth motion and at the same angle each time. To do this position your file on either the left or right side of the blade and as you push the file downwards move to the opposite side.

For curved tools or for tools where the blade comes to a point in the middle, start the file from the center of the blade and file out towards one side. Then repeat for the opposite side. As a general rule you should always sharpen the front or top side of the blade.

The first time you file a new tool it will take 100-200 strokes to file the steel down to it's new angle. The number of strokes it takes to produce an edge depends on the hardness of the steel and how sharp your file is.

As you are forming the bevel on one side of the blade a thin wire will curl on the underside. Once you finish sharpening you should flip the tool over and holding the file at a 5 degree angle make a few light strokes to remove the wire. Try not to apply too much pressure on this side or you will dull the edge you've just created. Your only goal here is to remove the thin wire and that's it.

You should never sharpen any garden tool on both sides of the blade. The only tool that gets sharpened this way is a knife which is made from extremely hard steel. Without such a high quality steel the edge would dull quickly or break off during the sharpening process.

Generally gardening tools should all be sharpened at 15 degrees on the front side of the blade. For shovels it's the side that faces into the hole you are digging and for secateurs it's the side that faces out when the secateurs are closed. The only garden tool that should be sharpened differently is the hoe which works better when the blade is made at a 20 degree angle.

How To Prevent Your Tools From Rusting And Ensure They Last At Least 20 Years

When you invest in good quality tools it makes sense to look after them. After all you've just spent a considerable amount of money and time buying and sourcing them, so you want to make sure they last as long as possible!

It's easy to forget or postpone tool maintenance when there are so many things to do in your garden. One of the best things you can do is to create an easy to use tool cleaner that can be used on your tools every time you return them to the tool shed.

I have an old rag next to a solution of bleach, tea tree oil and water which I use for wiping and sterilizing cutting tools such as secateurs, snips and knives. After I've wiped my tools over I just hang them up to dry and whenever the spring gets a little stiff I give the joints a drop or two of machine oil.

The solution for sterilizing your secateurs, knives and snips is:

- *1 part bleach*
- *1 part tea tree oil*
- *10 parts water*

Mix thoroughly in a mason jar and store with the lid closed.

For larger tools like shovels, forks and hoes I have a bucket next to the door which is filled with coarse sand soaked in linseed oil. Every time I bring my tools back from the yard I brush off any dirt from them and then plunge the blades around in the bucket of oily sand.

The sand helps keep the edge sharpened and cleans the metal of any finer dirt. Whilst the oil applies a protective coating to the steel to prevent it from rusting.

After cleaning the tool heads I grab an old cloth and dip it into some linseed oil and use it to rub the wooden handles. If you do this every time you use your tools you'll never have to worry about split handles because the oil keeps the wood flexible. The oil also protects the wood from getting wet and swelling, which is the main cause of handles coming loose from the tool head. When the wood gets wet it stretches and bends the steel around the handle, so when the wood dries out and shrinks it ends up being loose in the fitting.

How I clean my shovels, hoes and forks:

1. Remove soil and sod with a stiff wire brush
2. Plunge tool heads into the bucket of sandy oil several times to clean them
3. Rub oil into the wooden handles using an old rag
4. Every few months sharpen the cutting edge of your tools with a file

With regular maintenance your tools should last upwards of 20 years. Opa's has had most of his for more than 50 years and they are still going strong!

Remember To Download Your Free Book Resources

As part of your purchase you've got access to exclusive book bonuses and extras. These include printable plans for the chicken tractor, the homemade fertilizer recipe, a quick start checklist to begin your first patch and many more free resources such as:

- Printable plant spacing tables
- List of recommended seed companies
- Natural pest management plants list
- Plans for building an insect hotel
- Plans for building a chicken tractor
- Printable homemade fertilizer recipe
- Beginners quick start checklist

Download or print your free bonuses now.

Visit www.obsessedwithdirt.com/resources

The Basics Of Sowing Seeds That Germinate Reliably

I had been trying for weeks to get seeds to grow in my garden. A few had come up alright but most of the seeds I'd sown hadn't germinated at all.

So when I visited Opa's vegetable garden I was surprised to see he had hundreds of young seedlings growing directly in his beds. It was still the first few weeks of spring, yet Opa was already harvesting early crops of radish, lettuce and beans, he even had a dozen tomato plants growing happily despite the cool weather.

"I've been waiting for you" he said as I knelt down to examine a row of young seedlings opening their first leaves to the morning sun.

"How are you getting your seeds to germinate so early? I can't get any to sprout in my garden!" I exclaimed.

I explained all the different things I was trying. The seed germination kits, seed raising potting mix, heat mats and all sorts of stuff to get my seeds started. Even though I had a little success from raising seeds in the plastic germination kits. When I transplanted them into the garden the seedlings quickly wilted and needed to be watered constantly to keep them perked up.

"You make it more complicated than it should be. The seeds want to grow, you just have to tell them it's time to wake up" he said as he shook his head and patted me on the back.

"C'mon, let me show you"

Opa walked over to his garden shed, picked up his bow rake and a jar filled with water and rocks. He swirled the water around in the jar as he walked in front of me.

Making a grinding noise as the rocks knocked loudly against each other in the jar.

"What with the jar of rocks Opa?" I asked with a puzzled look across my face.

"I'm calling upon the river to wake up my seeds"

The river? What on earth does Opa mean, it's just a jar filled with water and rocks. But as I watched the rocks swirl around I saw that it wasn't just rocks in the jar. There were hundreds of little seeds in there too.

"Aren't you damaging the seeds by swirling those rocks around?"

"Yes. I told you, the seeds need to wake up. They have a hard protective shell that keeps them safe for many years. When the river floods the stones break apart the hard shell, waking the seeds up and telling them it's time to grow"

We continued walking through his vegetable garden until we got to a bare bed. The chickens had been here only a few days ago and the soil was all scratched up and fluffy. There was a little left uncomposted debris on the top of the soil, which Opa raked onto the path as he evened out the soil in the bed.

Kneeling down he grabbed his rake and pressed the handle lightly into the fluffy soil, leaving a furrow across the bed. He roughly measured and stamped furrows into the bed until all the row was mapped out in neat rows.

Grabbing the jar he removed the rocks and strained off the water. Leaving only the swollen seeds in the bottom. Then he tapped the seeds out of the jar and into the first furrow on the garden bed. Some of the seeds were grouped too closely so he brushed them apart briskly with his fingers and continued tapping the seeds out into the furrows until all the jar was empty.

Using the back of his rake he lightly covered the seeds with soil before pressing the handle over the furrow once again. This time he pressed down firmly compacting the soil around the seeds and leaving a half inch deep depression across the bed.

"No water until they wake up" he said sternly as he packed up his things and walked back to the tool shed. When I returned in a few days the rows of seeds were thick with seedlings and it looked like almost every seed germinated.

Opa's method of germinating seeds is still the most reliable way to start crops that I know. After he showed me how to easily germinate seeds I threw out all the fancy seed raising kits and now sow everything by seed, directly into the garden beds.

The reason most gardeners have trouble getting their seeds to germinate is because they don't wake up their seeds before they sow them. All annual plants like vegetables and grains, have hard shells that protect their seeds during dry years.

The hard casing will not allow the seed to germinate until there is enough water available for the plant to grow. Just pushing the seeds into the soil and watering is not enough to reliably wake up most seeds.

Annual seeds need to be soaked for 6-24 hours immediately before you sow them. To increase germination it's a good idea to also lightly scarify the seeds by deliberately damaging the hard casing. This opens up the seed casing and lets the seed absorb water and ultimately germinate. Opa did this by swirling around a few rocks in the jar of water, but you can also lightly sand the seeds with sandpaper or knick them with a knife if that's more your style.

Once the hard casing is broken the seed will quickly swell and absorb water. You might even see the seed begin to sprout in the jar. If you see this then you should plant your seeds as soon as you can, rather than waiting the full 24 hours. Smaller seeds won't need to be soaked for as long as larger seeds, but you can safely soak all vegetable seeds for up to 24 hours without damaging the seeds.

Next you'll want to prepare your garden beds by removing any debris from the surface and also rake the top 1-2 inches of soil to make sure it's a fine crumbly consistency. Having a crumbly soil will help the bed warm up faster and reduces the chance of seeds rotting from overly wet soils.

As a rule, seeds should be sown 1-2 times the depth of the seed that is being sown. Most small seeds only need to be sprinkled across the soil, whereas larger seeds such as squash or beans should be pushed ¼ to ½ inch into the dirt.

Next you'll want to compact the soil immediately around your seeds. This is an important step because compacted soil forms a capillary channel in your garden. Ensuring that your seeds always have plenty of moisture available whilst they are germinating.

This is the reverse of the principle we discuss earlier. The loosened soil in the garden bed breaks the capillary channels to reduce evaporation, but when we compact a small area of the loosened soil we restore the capillary channel to the furrow. This creates a 'wick' that attracts moisture from the surrounding soil and subsoils. If you do this, you'll always find that your seed furrows are consistently moist throughout the day which greatly increases germination.

The final and very important step is to *not* water your seeds after you have sown them. If you live in a dry area then you should water your soil 1-2 days before sowing your seeds to prime the available water stored in the garden bed, but otherwise don't apply any water until your seeds have germinated.

This is important because the soaked seeds already have all the water they need to germinate inside their swollen shells. All your seeds need now is warm soil to bring them to life. If you water your soil you decrease the temperature of the garden bed and slow the growth of your seeds. Cold soil is the single biggest cause of low or failed germination.

After your seeds have grown their first true leaves then you can water them *if* they need it. Chances are you won't need to water your seedlings for most of the first month because there will be plenty of water stored in your soil. By reducing how often you water, you'll increase the rate at which your crops grow because the soil will be warmer.

When you sow your seeds always sow 3-5 times more seeds than you think you'll need. After the seeds grow their first true leaves snip off the weakest seedlings leaving 2-3 clumped together. It's better to cut the young seedlings off at the base then pull them because pulling them can damage the roots of the seedlings you want to keep.

After your crops grow a few more weeks you'll find that one of the 3 remaining seedlings grows much better than the other two. It'll be larger, healthier and growing faster than the others. When you can clearly see a superior grower then snip off the remaining seedlings.

This might seem wasteful at first but seeds are incredibly cheap. Most gardeners only use about 1/10th of the seeds in the packet before the seeds get too old to germinate reliably. What ends up happening is that most of the seeds just get thrown away when the packet expires.

When you over sow your vegetable seeds you replicate what happens in nature. Vegetables produce a lot of seeds at the end of the season, sometimes hundred of thousands of seeds per plant. When the following season comes all these seeds are forced to compete against each other and only the strongest win.

This is a very powerful way to grow crops that are resilient and fast growing. If you over sow and thin every year, then save the seeds from the healthiest crop you'll quickly create your own strain of incredibly healthy and easy to grow crops.

What About Transplanting Seedlings?

Avoid buying or starting seedlings as much as you can. Store bought seedlings are a waste of money. They are always root bound and almost always grown from weak varieties that are easy targets for pests and diseases.

The first thing seeds do *before* they push their little leaves up out of the dirt is to grow a tap root as far down into the soil as they can manage. Within 2 days of germinating most vegetables will have a tap root 2-3 inches deep into your soil. The main purpose of this root is to ensure your new seedling never runs goes thirsty. This is why directly sown seeds rarely need to be watered during their first month of growth.

However, when you germinate seeds in punnets and then transplant them into the soil you destroy the plants tap root. Just take one look at the curled mess of roots at the bottom of any seedling and you'll see just how silly the idea of transplanting seedlings is.

By the time you plant the seedling in the ground it's already too late to grow the tap root. The plant is now focused on growing feeder roots to collect nutrients for its leaves. This is why transplanted seedlings wilt unless watered regularly. They have missed the important first stage of growth and will *never* grow a strong tap root to collect water.

Furthermore, seedlings are grown from low quality vegetable varieties. Nurseries select varieties with the highest germination rates and sow the least seeds possible per punnet. Seedlings don't have to compete with each other and instead every seed regardless of how strong and healthy it is, grows up into a marketable seedling.

This is why garden centers can sell seedlings so cheaply. They know that once you have these sickly plants that are destined to fail, you'll be back in their store buying all sorts of fertilizers and sprays as you try to keep them alive.

Commercial seedlings are weak, low yielding and easy targets for pests and diseases. Home raised seedlings are better in that you have greater control over the varieties. However, they will still never grow into strong plants because the tap root never develops properly. Transplanted seedlings no matter what brand or techniques you use, will always have an increased dependence on water and nutrients to grow.

Some gardeners still choose to grow seedlings trying to get a jump start on the season. But whenever you transplant a seedling it always sends the plants into shock. Vegetables aren't used to being uprooted and having their growing conditions suddenly change.

When a seedling gets watered at the same time every day, has plenty of chemical fertilizers and perfectly sterile growing medium it gets used to that environment. Transplanting seedlings into real dirt, with real bugs and bacteria creates a huge stress on the plant.

Roots are not used to pushing through the unfamiliar soil that is now all around them. Having their reliable watering schedule changed, causes the young plants to stop growing for several weeks as they try to conserve resources and figure out what's going on.

Seedling growers use temperature controlled greenhouses permanently set to a comfortable 75°F

(24℃). When moved to the garden center seedlings can sit on the shelf for up to a month in shock. This is great for nurseries because the plants stop growing which means they can hold onto them for weeks before they have to get rid of them.

When you move your plants out into the garden beds they get shocked again. This time it's because of all the soil bacteria and microbes that they are not used to. If you're raising seedlings to plant out early in the spring, your little seedlings will be significantly slower growers than crops sown direct from seed.

Transplanted seedlings have slower growth over the whole season because of their compromised root systems. The first few months seedlings will hardly grow at all. Whereas direct sown crops shoot up like crazy for the first few weeks, and then continue to grow strong for the rest of the season.

Whenever I've planted seedlings and seeds at the same time the plants sown directly from seed have always outpaced the growth of the transplanted seedlings. There really is not advantage to raising seedlings and transplanting them. Whenever possible always directly sow seeds into your garden beds.

Where To Get The Best Vegetable Seeds

Nowadays you can buy vegetable seeds in practically every store from Wholefoods, Walmart and Kmart, to your local garden center. But the seeds that you see on these shelves are *not* the seeds you want to use to grow your vegetables.

If the seed packet costs more than the seeds it contains then you should probably find another seed supplier! Seed packets that have colorful and elaborate covers with glossy images and seemingly everything you need to know on the packet are designed to lure in amateur gardeners.

The seeds these well marketed packets contain are the lowest quality seeds on the market. They are the seeds that get sorted and rejected from the commercial trade either for being too old, damaged, small, or because they have terrible germination rates.

What's worse is that the seeds almost never grow true to type because they are a mix of similar varieties and not any one particular strain. This is why the packet will usually only be labelled as "green string beans" and even if a variety is named, the seed company knows that the average gardener won't be able to tell if the crops grow true to type or not. These seeds are unregulated and a complete waste of money.

You'll often find these seed packets sitting dusty on the shelves. They even might be out of date when you buy them because so few gardeners buy their seeds this way. Seed varieties are also limited and often not the best varieties for your area. Instead they are whatever the seed company can buy cheaply from seed wholesalers that year. These seeds germinate unreliably and produce low yields and poor quality crops.

Instead, buy your seeds the same place professional growers do. From the regulated farm supply seed companies. These companies are held to much higher regulatory standards because farmers are relying on their seeds to make a profit. If their seeds don't germinate reliably, grow slow or have low yields, then farmers will move their business elsewhere.

When evaluating which seed company to use, the first measure you should be looking at is the expected germination rates. All the best seed companies will tell you exactly how many of that particular variety of seed you need to sow to get 1 seed to germinate. They need to provide this information and it needs to be 100% accurate, because commercial farmers are relying on it to sow their crops at the correct spacings.

Good seed companies will also tell you exactly what different varieties needs to germinate reliably. Some seeds need light to germinate whilst others need complete darkness. All of this information should be easily found on the seed packet or webpage of the variety you are sowing. If it isn't then you should use another seed company.

Heirloom seeds are my preference for seeds, however I'm not against growing hybrids. Many backyard gardeners mistake hybrids for genetically modified crops which they are not. Hybrids are created from very careful and deliberate crossings between two varieties to create a seed that produces a reliable and marketable quality. This quality usually only lasts for one life cycle and the second generation of plants will revert back to growing more like one of the crossed varieties.

Occasionally I find a hybrid with exceptional quality, it might have very fast growth or a significant resistance to disease or pests. Even varieties with an especially tasty harvest are all great reasons to grow hybrid seeds.

Ultimately the best place to get your vegetable seed is from your own vegetable garden. With each generation your crops adjust to your local environment and growing conditions. After a few years the seeds you've saved will be specialists at thriving in your garden and will out grow any seed you by from a company.

However, because your vegetable garden is likely to be small. The species diversity is also likely to be small because you'll only grow 1-2 varieties of each crop at a time. Over time your seeds will get weaker as they become more inbred because there isn't enough genetic diversity in your patch. That's why it's important to introduce a new strain to your garden every 5-7 years to refresh the gene pool of your crops.

Bringing in a new variety is important because it adds new genetic code to your crops gene pool. These new genetic building blocks help protect your plant from unknown, new and evolving pest and diseases, that may be spreading across the country but not yet in your backyard. When they do happen to reach your yard your crops will already have the code to defend against them and will be much more resilient at fighting against them.

Saving seed is one of the easiest and most rewarding activities. All you have to do is select one plant that has the characteristics you want, let it go to seed and then sow the seed next season. It's really that easy!

When selecting plants to collect seed I usually select for one or more of these traits:

- Pest and disease resistance
- Ability to grow with minimal water and nutrients
- Fast growth
- Cold or heat tolerance
- Yield quality or quantity

For the best germination rates always store your seeds in an airtight container in the refrigerator with 1-2 packets of silica or storage desiccants. Fridges are ideal for seed storage as the consistently cold temperature keeps seeds in hibernation and the dark, dry environment keeps the seeds protected.

You can find a list of seed companies that I recommend in the online book resources available at www.obsessedwithdirt.com/resources

How To Eliminate Pests and Diseases From Your Garden Without Using Any Chemicals

Pests were never a problem in Opa's vegetable garden, diseases weren't common either. Yet, Opa didn't do anything to control or deter them. Pests and diseases were so rare that it wasn't even worth his time.

Occasionally he'd spot a caterpillar on a cabbage leaf and would pick them off and feed them to his chickens. Of course the chickens loved eating the tasty little treats but most of the time Opa would just leave them on his cabbages. His cabbages seemed to have no problem getting rid of them all by themselves.

Although I had closely followed everything Opa had taught me my vegetable garden was always overrun with pests. I tried so hard to not use chemicals but fighting the pests with organic sprays wasn't very effective. When I explained it to Opa he flashed his cheeky grin and said

"The trouble is, your good bugs are *starving*"

"You keep killing their dinner before they get to eat it. The bad bugs just move on to another leaf but the good bugs are starving"

"You want more bugs in your garden, not less"

Opa was right. If I had more good bugs eating the bad bugs, I wouldn't need to do anything to keep them under control. The good bugs would do it all for me! But how could I encourage more good bugs into my garden without losing my crops to pests?

Planted all around Opa's vegetable garden was a 3 foot

wide garden bed filled with dozens of flowering shrubs and herbs. When he ran his hands through the shrubs hundreds of insects of all shapes and sizes burst out in every direction. He had planted these shrubs to bring the good bugs back into his yard.

Once the shrubs were there the good bugs came back and he didn't have to spray his crops, not even with homemade or organic remedies. Instead he left the bad bugs to their natural predators, the good bugs who were now thriving in the bushes around his yard. Whenever a pest showed up in his garden the good bugs quickly came in and ate their favorite snack.

If pests got out of control, Opa would never interfere or try to fix the problem. He trusted his good bugs to do their job and protect his crops. In exchange he would provide them with all the shelter, water and food they needed to survive.

Occasionally, the pests would win the battle and kill a plant but Opa never worried about it. He saw it not as losing a plant, but as putting on a banquet for his good bugs to enjoy. The attacked plant was probably a bad strain anyway and wouldn't yield much, so why not give it to his army of good bugs to enjoy.

Thinking back to the river where Opa introduced me to the wild vegetables. The banks where the vegetables grew were covered thickly on both sides with flowering shrubs just like those in Opa's garden.

There were hundreds of different insects and creatures living near the river too from lizards, birds and worms, to dragonflies and ladybugs. The river was teaming with life and provided the perfect habitat for the good bugs to thrive.

Opas favorite plants to bring back the good bugs were:

- Dill
- Angelica

- Fennel
- Queen Anne's lace
- Cosmos
- Fern leaf yarrow
- Prairie sunflower
- Marigolds
- Tansy
- Vetch
- Golden marguerite
- Four wing saltbush
- You can use most other herbs and cottage plants as well, although the ones above are the most effective for encouraging good bugs

These plants give good bugs somewhere to nest and the abundant flowers provide food for them when there are no bad bugs to munch on. The best way to protect your crops is to plant the entire perimeter of your vegetable garden with these flowering plants. A narrow bed about 2 feet wide is all you need.

Having a perimeter of plants filled with good bugs makes it nearly impossible for bad bugs to reach your crops. First they'd have to get past the bushes filled with bugs that desperately want to eat them. If they manage to get to your crops, the good bugs will have followed them all the way from the moment they flew into your yard.

Encouraging good bugs back into your garden may take a while to do. In most areas all the good bugs have been completely wiped out by the insecticides sprayed on crops. One of the best ways to get started is to collect bugs from a nearby river or to buy them live online, and reintroduce them into your garden.

Pests will have the upper hand initially because they are more resistant to chemicals. However, if you continue to work with your good bugs they'll quickly start to keep your pests under control for you.

It's also a good idea to mimic other parts of the river to help insects thrive in your garden. Create small ponds of water and piles of sticks and debris, to provide additional habitats to your vegetable garden. You can even build insect hotels which are fantastic ways to encourage and support good bugs in your garden.

You can find a printable list of beneficial plants and plans for making your own insect hotels at the book resources page www.obsessedwithdirt.com/resources

Rotating Your Crops To Increase Yields

The same crop should never be grown in the same garden bed two years in a row. Each crop works the soil differently and also has a different nutrient load. If you grow the same crop in the same garden bed year after year, you will exhaust the soil of certain nutrients that the crop is a heavy feeder of.

But there is another reason to rotate your crops, and that's to control pests and diseases. Crops that are grown in the same spot have to work harder to mine the soil for the nutrients they need to grow and often won't get all the nutrients they need which makes them susceptible to attacks.

Many pests and diseases can overwinter in the soil, which means they'll already be there when you plant the same crop next year. If pests and diseases already have a foothold over the area, then your young seedlings have very little chance of thriving.

Traditional crop rotation separates plants into 4 groups based on their growth habits such as roots, fruits, leaves and misc. Although simple, this rotation system is flawed in that it doesn't take into account vegetables that are closely related but in different groups, such as tomatoes and potatoes.

Crops from the same plant family tend to be attacked by the same pests and diseases which is why it is better to group crops by the 8 major vegetable families. These families are:

- Brassicas - cabbages of all types, broccoli, cauliflower, brussel sprouts, kohlrabi, kale, mizuna, pak choi, radish, rocket, swede and turnips
- Legumes - peanuts, beans and peas
- Solanaceae - aubergine, potato, tomato, peppers
- Alliums - onions, garlic, chives, shallot, leeks
- Umbelliferae - celery, celeriac, coriander, fennel, carrot, parsnip, parsley, dill
- Cucurbits - courgette, cucumber, melons, pumpkins, squash
- Chenopodiaceae - swiss chard, spinach, beetroot
- Miscellaneous - herbs, okra, green manures

The above list is in the order that you should rotate your crops in. Start new garden beds with easy to grow plants from the chenopodiaceae family. These have deep roots that mine the subsoil and deposit large amounts of nutrients into the topsoil. They'll also help to break up new ground and open up compacted soil.

Cucurbits are a great crop to follow chenopodiaceae plants because they thrive in soils with high amounts of trace elements. They grow fast and provide shelter for insects and worms to come in and work the soil. Cucurbits require plenty of water to thrive, but don't need a lot of nutrients to grow well. They are best planted in mounds where the soil stays warm and dry rather than cool and damp. After they finish growing the worms and bugs will have worked the compost in the soil into a fine tilth which sets the stage for the next crop.

Umbelliferae need a rich topsoil to grow well which is why they do so well after cucurbits. They also have deep roots that explore deeply into the soil and fill the topsoil with plenty of trace minerals. These plants generally have thick taproots, which do an excellent job of breaking open compacted soil in preparation for alliums. Umbelliferae are heavy feeders and do a great job of absorbing excess nutrients in the soil, which encourages alliums to grow bigger roots in search of food.

Alliums are very powerful crops that exude phytochemicals into the soil. These chemicals are excellent at repelling nematodes and other pests. Their roots are shallow and matted which restricts them to using the nutrients in mostly the top 6 inches of the soil. If nematodes are a problem in your garden then try to leave as many allium roots in the soil as possible. This will increase the phytochemicals in the soil and discourage pests for many months after the onions have been harvested. Alliums will produce small bulbs if the soil is too rich, but grow big sweet bulbs when the soil is rich in trace minerals. This is why they do so well after umbelliferae.

Solanaceae will have increased pest resistance from all the phytochemicals left in the soil by the alliums. These phytochemicals are especially good at deterring the majority of solanaceae pests, especially nematodes. Solanaceae are heavy feeders and will produce huge crops if fertilized regularly. They generally leave a bed exhausted of nutrients which is why legumes follow them in our rotation.

Legumes naturally harvest nitrogen from the air and fix it into the soil. This is made possible by a special symbiotic relationship they have with soil microbes on their roots. They will restore and enrich the soil after the heavy feeding solanaceae crops and are resistant to solanaceae pests. When removing the legumes at the end of the season try to keep as much of the roots in the soil as possible, this will give your hungry brassicas an extra boost of slow release nitrogen.

Brassicas are the hungriest of all vegetable crops and require high levels of nitrogen to grow well. Many of the previous crop families have deposited trace minerals and exudates into the soil at this point, creating a rich stew for your brassicas. Keep them regularly fertilized and apply extra kelp meal to protect your crops against cabbage moths.

After brassicas your garden soil will be thoroughly worn out and in need of a rest. At this point you can turn it over to an assortment of herbs, which are great at concentrating trace minerals in the soil. They're also good at pumping the soil full of more phytochemicals to remove any lingering pests and diseases.

You could also grow crops with low fertilizer needs such as Jerusalem artichokes, okra or another round of legumes. It's also a good time to let the soil rest for a season and grow a green manure crop. Make sure you harvest the green manure before it goes to seed or the plants will take more nutrients out of the soil than they add. Green manures should be dig in and composted in the soil. The best way to do this is with your chicken tractor. Just cut the green manure and then let your chickens work it into the soil for you.

One of the only crops I haven't included in the rotation plan above is corn. That's because it is in the poaceae family which includes all grains like wheat, barley and rye. These crops are exceptionally heavy feeders. We've bred them to produce unnaturally large quantities of seeds that require a lot of energy to grow. Grains can quickly strip the soil of nutrients and are are very hungry feeders which is why I usually avoid growing them. If you want to grow corn or grains then do so instead of brassicas in the rotation above and follow with legumes or a green manure.

Some gardeners find rotating crops to be quite difficult. It can easily get confusing when you have to try and remember which crop follows who. The easiest way to setup your crop rotation is to divide your garden beds into 8 roughly equal blocks. If you've got 4 garden beds that's 2 blocks each to make 8 blocks total.

Once you've divided your beds into blocks then number them 1-8 and grow one vegetable family in each block for one season. As your crops mature and are removed plant the bed with the next family in the rotation. I find it's easiest to keep records in my garden journal so I'm always rotating my crops consistently.

7 Amazingly Easy Vegetables That You Can Grow Even If You've Got Brown Thumbs

When it comes to growing vegetables, not all crops are created equal. Some require constant tending, pruning and training to yield a decent harvest. Whilst others require little more than throwing a few seeds down and returning in a few weeks to fill your basket with food.

Here are the easiest vegetables to grow for beginner gardeners, particularly when you first start your vegetable garden. After a few years you garden will be a rich loamy soil and you'll be able to grow the most demanding crops easily too. But if you're just starting out, stick to these easy to grow crops.

Radish

This was the first vegetable I ever grew. Boy was I surprised when I bit into the attractive red flesh. I had never had a radish before and was not expecting the strong peppery explosion.

What I love about radishes is that they grow so incredibly easily. You basically scatter the seeds on the soil, water in and then harvest them in 4-6 weeks time. The young leaves are also edible and a good replacement for greens. They can sometimes be a little tough, and are best eaten steamed or boiled with the stems removed.

Tomatoes

Everyone loves homegrown tomatoes and it's easy to see why after you've popped one that's ripened on the vine into your mouth. Tomatoes are very easy to grow, especially the small cherry varieties which are highly resistant to pests and diseases.

To get the most fruit, you should pick off the side shoots as the plant grows. These are the little shoots that grow between the leaf and the main trunk. If you leave them on, the plant will spend more of its energy growing leaves and less on producing fruits. You can still get a decent crop without picking these shoots off, but the increased yields are well worth the effort.

Be sure to stake your tomatoes, or grow them in a cage to provide plenty of support from the heavy fruits as they grow. This is especially important later in the season when the plants can get very heavy with ripening fruits.

Lettuce

Store bought greens are very expensive and boring to eat. The leaves of lettuce spoil quickly once picked which is why all the lettuce at the green grocery is laced with chemicals. The chemicals keep the leaves crunchy, but are also fairly toxic to consume so make sure you rinse your store bought greens before you eat them.

Growing your own lettuce is much easier and safer than buying greens at the store. Sow seeds directly into the garden bed and in a few weeks you'll have lettuce ready to harvest. When you thin your seedlings you can eat the baby lettuce in salads, it's especially sweet and has a unique flavor. Lettuce needs to grow quickly or it will become bitter, so make sure you fertilize a few weeks after the plants germinate and keep them well watered to prevent bolting.

Potatoes

The easiest vegetable you could possible grow is the humble potato. You don't even need to buy any seeds! Just put a potato out in the sun for a few days until it starts to sprout and then bury it in your garden bed. In a few weeks it'll burst out of the soil producing a big green bush.

Mound soil up around the plant as it grows, leaving about 4 inches of leaves exposed at the top. When the leaves turn from green to yellow, the plant has finished growing. Carefully dig up the potatoes with a fork. Leave them in the sun for a few hours to dry, then pack them into sacks and keep in a dark place. You should grow about 10-20 potatoes from every tuber you plant.

Cucumber

These fast growers produce continuous crops of juicy fruits over the whole growing season. You can grow cucumbers up a trellis or just leave them to trail over the soil. The smaller cukes are easiest to grow and most productive.

Make sure you pick all the cucumbers that are ripe, as leaving any on the vine and the plant will stop producing. It's easy to miss the cucumbers hiding under leaves, so if you're vine isn't producing heavily take a good look to find the few you've missed. Cut these off and in a few weeks you'll be back to full production.

Squash

Be careful of where you plant this super productive vegetable. Just one plant can easily cover 100 sq ft in your vegetable garden. You'll have more squash than you'll know what to do with so get ready!

The flowers and young shoots are also edible and are best eaten fried in butter. If your garden soil is fairly damp then make sure you lift the squash off of the ground. If you leave them on damp soil they'll begin to rot long before they're ready to harvest. You can place small plant pots under the squash or mound them up slightly with course sand.

Zucchini

Get ready to put zucchini in everything because once this plant starts producing it doesn't stop! I've harvested 100's of zucchini from one plant over the season, and it showed no signs of slowing down. I had to put zucchini in everything for months!

It grows so fast that you can even watch it grow on the vine. Just sneak out to your patch at night with a torch after a warm summer's day and you'll see the zucchini expanding out before your eyes!

How To Maintain Your Vegetable Garden For Increased Yields and Save Hours Of Work

Although Opa loved being out in his vegetable garden he never wanted to do any more work than he had to. Over the years he came up with many great ideas to save himself time and money. It also helped him grow an incredible amount of food from very little effort and resources.

The biggest time consuming task is setting up a new vegetable garden, but after you've done the hard work once it's done. All that's left is a little ongoing maintenance throughout the season to keep improving your soil.

Whereas most gardeners waste their time on things like making composts and digging over beds, Opa never spent much time with these tasks. Instead, he hired animals to do these things for him and they did are far better job than he could ever hope to do!

About the only work left was sowing seeds and then training and harvesting the crops. This work was made even easier by using well designed and regularly sharpened tools.

Opa spent only a handful of hours a week maintaining his big 1200 sq ft vegetable garden, whereas other intensive gardeners could easily spend 20 or more hours in the same area and still not produce as much food as what he did.

Here's how he took care of his garden:

1. Take a stroll once a week with your quick action hoe in hand and run it over all the bare earth in

the garden beds. This helps keeps moisture in the soil and eliminates weeds

2. Check your soils moisture levels once a week and apply up to 1 inch of additional water as needed, make sure you hoe the beds again afterwards to reduce evaporation

3. Rake in a little homemade fertilizer around hungry crops or plants that are showing signs of pests or diseases once a fortnight. The nutrients in the fertilizer will help the plant fight back against the attack.

4. Train your crops up trellises and harvest produce *daily*. It's important to do this daily as it will increase your yields considerably

5. Remove crops that have finished production leaving most of the roots in the soil. Rake the garden bed level and wait a week for the worms to start cleaning up the bed

6. Move the chicken tractor to the bed to get the chickens working on fluffing up and composting the soil.

7. Chop up all the garden waste from the other beds and feed it into your chicken tractor to enrich the bed with nutrients. Leave the tractor on the bed until the next bed needs to be worked over.

8. Rake off the remaining debris from the garden bed and sow your next crop directly in the bed from seeds

9. If you have any garden beds that you don't currently need to use or whenever you have a gap between planting your next crop cover the soil with a green manure. Then 1 week before you need the bed move the chicken tractor onto the green manure to clear and prepare the bed for you.

10. As soon as your good bug plants finish flowering cut them back to about 1 foot high and wide. Feed them with some fertilizer and add the garden waste to your chicken tractor. Only prune back a few at a time otherwise you'll lose your population of good bugs.

Thank You

By now you should have a clear idea of how to grow vegetables the easy way. Hopefully after reading this book you'll be able to avoid many of the costly traps that vegetable gardeners fall into.

Learning to grow my own vegetables has been a great journey. It's brought me closer to my Opa, helped provide nutritious food for my family and kept me physically healthy too.

I know that if you follow the simple methods we've discussed in this book that you'll be able to grow your own vegetables in your own backyard too. The best part is that you won't have to buy any expensive equipment or spend thousands on fertilizers, composts or chemicals to do it.

You've just learned how to grow practically anything you want, using simple techniques and organic fertilizers that you can readily source anywhere in the world.

I'd love to hear about your vegetable gardening success and help you grow more food organically, if you'd like to get in touch with me then email book@obsessedwithdirt.com or visit us at www.obsessedwithdirt.com

Please Leave A Review

Did you enjoy this book?

If so then please take a minute to leave a review and tell other backyard gardeners about it! Every review helps this book get seen by more gardeners. Your review might even inspire someone to start growing their first vegetable garden!

Click here to leave a review on Amazon.

Thanks so much!

Mitch

Remember To Download Your Free Book Resources

As part of your purchase you've got access to exclusive book bonuses and extras. These include printable plans for the chicken tractor, homemade fertilizer recipe, a quick start checklist to begin your first patch and many more free resources.

Plus you'll get unreleased bonuses that aren't in this book including:

- Printable plant spacing tables
- List of recommended seed companies
- Natural pest management plants list
- Plans for building an insect hotel
- Plans for building a chicken tractor
- Printable homemade fertilizer recipe
- Beginners quick start checklist

Download or print your free bonuses now.

Visit www.obsessedwithdirt.com/resources